NUTSHELLS

CONSTITUTIONAL AND ADMINISTRATIVE LAW IN A NUTSHELL

FOURTH EDITION

by

Greer Hogan, LL.B., M.A.
Deputy Head of the Law School (Academic)
University of Northumbria at Newcastle

London ● Sweet & Maxwell ● 1996

Published in 1996 by
Sweet & Maxwell Limited of
100 Avenue Road, Swiss Cottage, London, NW3 3PF
http:/www.smlawpub.co.uk
Phototypeset by
Wyvern Typesetting Limited, Bristol
Printed in England by Clays Ltd, St Ives plc

Reprinted 1998

A CIP Catalogue record
for this book is available
from the British Library

ISBN 0–421–548509

CONTENTS

1. THE NATURE OF THE CONSTITUTION

Most countries have a written document known as "the constitution" which lays down the main rules governing the structure and functions of government and which regulates the relationship between the state and its citizens. Typically such constitutions are to some degree entrenched, that is, the constitutional rules are more difficult to change than ordinary laws, perhaps requiring approval by referendum (Republic of Ireland) or special majority (United States of America). Such constitutions also tend to have a higher status than ordinary laws thus creating the need for a supreme body such as a supreme court with the power to declare laws passed in contravention of the constitution, invalid.

CHARACTERISTICS OF THE BRITISH CONSTITUTION

Unwritten
In Britain we do not have a written constitution in the sense of a formal document but that does not mean that we lack constitutional rules. These are expressed with differing degrees of formality in the form of statutory provisions, case law and conventions of the constitution.

There are, compared to many countries, few positive statements regarding the powers and duties of the organs of government. These are simply recognised by common law and convention and are subject to various legal and conventional limitations. Our constitution does not contain any positive declaration of the rights of individuals in the form of a Bill of Rights. Those rules relating to such matters as freedom of speech and assembly derive from, and have the same status as, any other rule of law.

Flexible
The British Constitution can be described as flexible in that:

(a) It does not have the rigidity of most written constitutions as Parliament can repeal any law by a simple majority. The orthodox viewpoint is that, as each successive Parliament has the power to pass or repeal any legislation, any attempt to bind Parliament by entrenching a statutory provision, would be ineffective. (*Ellen Street*

Estates Ltd. v. Minister of Health (C.A., 1936).) It has, however, been argued that certain fundamental Acts of Parliament such as the Act of Union with Scotland 1707 and the European Communities Act 1972 could not be repealed as, in each case, Parliament which enacted the provision is no longer in existence in the same form but has reconstituted itself as a less powerful body.

Nevertheless, while in legal theory there may be complete flexibility, the political reality may be quite different. The Statute of Westminster 1931, the various Independence Acts may, in theory, be capable of repeal, but in practice they are entrenched in our constitution. "Freedom once given cannot be taken away. Legal theory must give way to practical politics." (*Per* Lord Denning in *Blackburn v. The Att.-Gen.* (C.A., 1971).)

(b) The absence of a written constitution has allowed quite considerable changes to be made informally, without amendment of these legal rules which do exist. For example, the gradual transfer of power from the House of Commons to the Cabinet has occurred without any formal legislative change. Conventions, an important source of constitutional law can be extremely flexible, reflecting changes in the political situation as and when they occur. Thus the constitution can evolve gradually.

Unitary

Because all legislative power stems from Parliament, we have a unitary as opposed to a federal constitution. It is certainly possible for Parliament to give limited powers of government to local authorities and to local and national assemblies but the doctrine of parliamentary sovereignty means that a subsequent Parliament can repeal the relevant legislation and take back the power. For example this happened in 1972 when the Westminster Parliament reimposed direct rule in Northern Ireland.

SOURCES OF THE CONSTITUTION

Legislation

Although we do not have a written constitution there are many Acts of Parliament relevant to constitutional laws. Some fundamental steps in the constitutional development of the country were the Bill of Rights 1689 which limited the power of the monarch to rule by virtue of the royal prerogative, the Act of Settlement 1700 which further strengthened the power of Parliament and provided for the succession to the English throne and the European Communities Act 1972 which took this country into what is now known as the European Union (E.U.). The composition of Parliament has been altered by the Peerage Act 1963 and its powers by the Parliament Acts 1911 and 1949.

Case law

According to Dicey, writing in the nineteenth century, the British Constitution was "judge made." Even today there are many areas of constitutional law regulated not by statute but by the common law as expounded by our judges. Examples of this can be seen in the development of the doctrine of the supremacy of Parliament and in judicial review, for example, the rules of natural justice.

In recent years there has been an increased reliance on statute law, for example, in relation to public order and the powers of the police, but, of course, here too, the judges have a role to play in the interpretation of the statutory provisions.

Conventions of the Constitution

If one tries to understand the British Constitution simply by reference to case law and statute, one obtains a totally false impression. Take one example, the role played by the monarch. The Queen must give the royal assent to all legislation. She appoints the Prime Minister and has the power to dissolve Parliament. This might lead one to believe that the monarch still exercises considerable political power. Yet in practice we now have a constitutional monarchy where the Queen acts on the advice of her Prime Minister. The royal assent has not been refused since 1708. No monarch has refused to dissolve Parliament in modern times and the Queen has, in recent years, been relieved of any real responsibility as to the choice of Prime Minister as the various political parties have now clearly defined rules for the election of a leader.

Such changes in the power of the monarch have arisen, not through statute, but as a result of the convention that the monarch should not become politically involved and should not be seen to favour any one political party.

This example illustrates the fact that the formal rules have to be understood against a background of constitutional conventions which can both expand and modify the strict legal rules. And so conventions have been described as "the flesh which clothes the dry bones of the law."

What are conventions?

(a) Conventions are non-legal rules of constitutional behaviour which are considered to be binding upon those who operate the constitution but which are not enforced by the courts or by the presiding officers in Parliament. They may be recognised by the courts as part of the constitutional background against which a particular decision is taken (*Carltona v. Commissioner of Works* (C.A., 1943)), but will not be enforced directly. (See also *Reference Re Amendment of the Constitution of Canada* (Supreme Court of Canada 1982).)

(b) They are not written down in any formal sense in that they are not expressed as Acts of Parliament nor are they established by judicial precedent. Occasionally an existing convention is formalised as, for example, section 43 of the Statute of Westminster 1931.

(c) Important constitutional institutions such as the Cabinet and the office of Prime Minister have been created by convention. The first statutory reference to the Prime Minister came in the Chequers Estate Act 1917. The relationship between Government and Parliament can only be understood against the background of the convention of ministerial responsibility. They thus have a central role in the development of the British Constitution.

Advantages and disadvantages of conventions

While the use of conventions can add flexibility to our constitutional rules and avoid the constant need for formal change to ensure the constitution properly reflects the realities of political life, it does provide the government with easy opportunities to amend the rules in its favour.

Other sources

The law of the European Union

By virtue of our membership of the European Union, community law is part of our law. The primary sources of community law are the Treaties, for example the three founding Treaties and the Treaty of European Union. The secondary sources are regulations, directives and decisions of the Council and the Commission and the jurisprudence of the European Court of Justice.

The law and custom of Parliament

Parliament has the right to regulate its own procedure and does so by means of standing orders. These, together with resolutions passed by either House and the rulings given by the Speaker, are contained in Erskine May's *Parliamentary Practice*.

Treaties, Conventions and other international obligations

These are not a direct source of constitutional law in the sense that they do not normally involve any change in domestic law (see, however *The Parlement Belge* (H.C., 1879)). A treaty may bind the government in international law but will normally be given effect within this country by the passing of legislation. This happened in the case of membership of the EC where the signing of the various treaties was followed by the passing of the European Communities Act 1972. Similarly international conventions such as the International Convention for the Protection of Human Rights 1950, ratified by Great Britain in 1953, do not give directly enforceable rights to individuals in this country before the British courts (See *R v. Home Secretary ex p. Brind* (H.L., 1991)). The courts will, however, have some regard for such conventions presuming that Parliament intended to comply with its moral obligations and bring our law into line with the convention. Thus, for example, where there is any ambiguity in domestic law the courts have said that they will resolve that ambiguity in such a way as to give effect to our international obligations. (See Scarman L.J. in *Ahmad v. I.L.E.A.* (C.A., 1978).)

A finding by the Court of Human Rights that a law of the U.K. Parliament does not accord with the provisions of the ECHR will not render that act invalid although there would be considerable political pressure on our Parliament to modify the legislation. This occurred after the *Sunday Times v. U.K.* (1979) case. The finding by the ECJ that our law on contempt contravened Article 10 of the E.C.H.R. led to reform. (Contempt of Court Act 1981.)

THE SUPREMACY OF PARLIAMENT

An important characteristic of our constitution has been that Parliament, not the constitution, was the supreme legal authority. While, in the majority of states, the legislature is limited by the constitution in what it can or cannot do, our Parliament has been subject to no such legal limitation. Our courts have no power to declare laws duly passed by Parliament invalid.

According to Blackstone "What Parliament doth, no power on earth can undo." "In theory," said Dicey, "Parliament has total power. It is sovereign."

Dicey's view of Parliamentary supremacy

(a) Parliament was competent to pass laws on any subject.

(b) Its laws could regulate the activities of anyone, anywhere.
(c) Parliament could not bind its successors as to the content, manner and form of subsequent legislation.
(d) Laws passed by Parliament could not be challenged by the courts.

The legal limitations on the scope of Parliament's power

Dicey argued that there was no legal limitation on the scope of Parliament's power. Indeed Parliament has legislated on matters affecting every aspect of our lives. It has legislated to change fundamental constitutional principles. It has lengthened and shortened its own life. Nor has it felt bound by territorial or jurisdictional limits. Parliament has legislated regarding aliens, even with regard to their activities outside British territory (The Hijacking Act 1967). Sir Ivor Jennings once said "If Parliament enacts that smoking in the streets of Paris is an offence then, in the eyes of the English Courts, it is an offence." There may be practical difficulties in enforcing such a law but that would not make it invalid.

Political considerations may make it unlikely, even inconceivable that Parliament might legislate in a particular manner. Can one imagine a situation where Parliament passed legislation regulating the internal affairs of the United States of America? This led Professor H. W. R. Wade to argue that it was nonsensical to have a legal theory which said that Parliament could pass laws on any subject without restriction. Certainly there are many internal and external political limitations on Parliament's freedom of action.

It has been argued that British membership of the EU imposes a legal not simply a political limitation on Parliament.

The 1967 White Paper (Cmnd. 3301) on the Legal and Constitutional Implications of Membership of the EC, stated that Parliament's freedom of action would be limited in that it would have to refrain from passing legislation inconsistent with community law and would be under an obligation in certain instances to legislate to give effect to our community obligations. The European Communities Act 1972, s.2(1) gives present and future community law legal force in the United Kingdom and s.2(2) provides for the implementation of community law by means of secondary legislation but the Act does not specifically prohibit Parliament from enacting conflicting legislation.

If, however, such conflicting legislation was ineffective in so far as it was inconsistent with community law, Parliament's power to legislate as it liked would be accordingly limited. McEldowney, for example, argues that such a limitation has occurred as Parliament's authority to legislate has become integrated with EC legislative policy. Certainly, in practical terms the increased co-operation required in the development of a common foreign and defence policy arising out of the Treaty on European Union and the emphasis on co-operation in home affairs is an ever increasing fetter on the Westminster Parliament's freedom of action.

The power of Parliament to bind its successors

The courts have long accepted Dicey's view that Parliament has no power to bind its successors either as to the manner or as to the form of subsequent legislation. As each successive Parliament is deemed to be all powerful, logically, that Parliament must have the power to make or unmake any law. Accordingly it would seem to be impossible to entrench a provision in our constitution.

It was said in *Godden v. Hales* (1686) that Parliament was entitled to ignore any provision in an earlier Act purporting to prevent the Act being repealed in the normal way, that is either expressly or by implication. This was followed in the case of *Ellen Street Estates Ltd. v. The Minister of Health* (C.A., 1934) where the court found that it was impossible for Parliament to enact that, in a subsequent statute dealing with the same subject-matter, there should be no implied repeal. "The one thing Parliament cannot do is to bind its successors" (Maughan L.J.).

Various arguments have been put forward to suggest that specific statutory provisions have been entrenched.

The Statute of Westminster: Independence Acts

It has been argued that these have been entrenched as, in terms of the political realities of the situation, it is inconceivable that Parliament would repeal them. (Lord Denning M.R. in *Blackburn v. The Att.-Gen.* (C.A., 1971).)

That is not to say that if, in the future, Parliament did repeal an Independence Act and passed legislation purporting to regulate the internal affairs of the country, the British courts would reject such legislation. In *Madzimbamuto v. Lardner Burke* (P.C., 1969) Lord Reid said that even if Parliament acted improperly or unwisely, it was not open to the courts to say that it had acted illegally and that the resultant legislation was invalid. The court advised that a detention order made under the authority of an Emergency Powers Act passed by the illegal regime in Rhodesia was invalid as its authority to legislate had been taken away. It did not allow the political reality of the situation to affect its conclusion knowing full well that the detention order would continue to be upheld within Rhodesia. In practical terms it was impossible to provide a remedy for the detained Madzimbamuto. The case did, of course, involve a limited grant of independence. Rhodesia was not a sovereign state.

Where such a sovereign state has been created by a grant of independence, the courts may be more reluctant to take back power in that they would have to recognise the political fact that the state in question was a foreign country and no longer part of the legal order of this country. Yet within our legal system, Parliament appears to have the legal power to repeal any law, even to act contrary to the principles of international law. The courts would simply uphold the latest intention of Parliament. (See Lord Sankey L.C. in *British Coal Corp. v. The King* (H.L., 1935) and Sir Robert Megarry V.-C. in *Manuel v. Attorney General* (H.C., 1983).)

The European Communities Act 1972

Several grounds have been suggested for holding that this Act cannot be repealed:

(a) That by joining the European Economic Community, a new order has been created. Within that new order Parliament is no longer all powerful and cannot amend or repeal any statute by which that order was established. The European Communities Act, it is argued, is such a constituent statute, and is accordingly entrenched.

(A similar argument has been used with regard to the Act of Union between Scotland and England in 1707.)

(b) That by assigning rights and powers to the community in accordance with the Treaty provisions member states have limited their sovereign rights in such a way as to make it impossible to withdraw unilaterally. (*Art Treasures Case* (E.C., 1972).)

There is no evidence to suggest that the British courts would accept this view. The political view is clearly that a right to withdraw exists.

(c) That, ultimately, the validity of legislation depends on the rules of recognition employed by our judges. The present norm of validity recognises the latest statutory intention of Parliament. It has been suggested that this norm has altered and that the courts will recognise as valid only legislation which has been passed by both houses and given the royal assent, has not been repealed expressly or by implication and which accords with our obligations under community law. (It has been suggested that one method by which a written constitution could be entrenched could be by "manufacturing" such a change in the norm of validity by altering the terms of the judicial oath so that judges would swear to uphold only laws which were in conformity with the constitutional provisions *per* H. W. R. Wade, 1989 Hamlyn Lecture: *Constitutional Fundamentals*.)

Laws passed by Parliament cannot be challenged in the courts

Traditionally our courts have refused to consider the validity of an Act of Parliament either on the ground that Parliament had no power to pass it or on the ground that the statute had been improperly passed.

Substantive validity

Until the seventeenth century the courts would declare Acts of Parliament void if they considered them contrary to natural law, repugnant to the law or impossible to be performed. In modern times any such challenge has been totally unsuccessful.

In *R. v. Jordan* (1967) Jordan, who had been sentenced for offences under the Race Relations Act 1965, applied for a writ of habeas corpus claiming that he had been convicted under an invalid law. He alleged that the statute in question was invalid in that it conflicted with a fundamental principle of natural law, the right of free speech. He claimed that no Act of Parliament could take away this right.

This was rejected by the court which simply stated that it had no power to consider the validity of an Act of Parliament. This view was endorsed by the House of Lords in *British Rail Board v. Pickin* (H.L., 1974) and followed in *Martin v. O'Sullivan* (C.A., 1982).

Procedural irregularity

Acts of Parliament have also been challenged on the ground that they have been improperly passed. In 1842 a Private Act of Parliament was challenged on this ground (*Edinburgh & Dalkeith Railway v. Wauchope* (H.L.,1842)). Lord Campbell, upholding the validity of the Act, refused to investigate the internal workings of Parliament saying that if the Act appeared valid on its face, then it must be accepted by the courts. If, from the Parliamentary Roll it appeared that the Bill had passed through both Houses and received the Royal Assent, the courts could not inquire into what happened during its parliamentary stages. That is a question for Parliament.

A number of writers have sought to distinguish such a procedural challenge from the substantive challenge in cases such as *Jordan* arguing that it does not seek to limit Parliament's area of power. It can be argued that there is a clear difference between finding that Parliament has failed to follow its own procedural rules and from saying that Parliament does not have the power to legislate in a particular way. R. F. V. Heuston summarises this by saying that there is a distinction between the rules which govern on the one hand the composition and the procedure and, on the other hand, the area of power, of a sovereign legislature.

The Judicial Committee of the Privy Council appeared to give some support to this distinction. In *Att.-Gen. for New South Wales v. Trethowan* (P.C., 1932) a decision of the Australian Supreme Court to grant a declaration that two Bills passed by the New South Wales State Legislature were invalid and grant an injunction restraining the Bills from being presented to the Governor for asset was upheld. The Privy Council found that the State Legislature was bound by section 5 of the Colonial Laws Validity Act 1865 which required any constitutional amendment to be in the manner and form required by the legislation in force at the time. The two Bills in question were not in the manner and form required as under earlier State legislation any constitutional change had to be approved by a referendum. (See also the South African case of *Harris v. Minister of the Interior* (1952).)

Membership of the EC—its effect on Parliamentary supremacy

In the view of the European Court, the courts of the Member States should give supremacy to Community law (*Costa v. E.N.E.L.*, 1964).

The 1967 White Paper on membership at paragraph 23, states the government's intention to be that "Community law takes precedence over the domestic law of the member states." Such an approach is necessary to ensure the necessary harmonisation of the laws of the member states.

Section 2(4) of the Act provides ". . . any enactment passed or to be passed, other than one contained in this Part of this Act, shall be construed and have effect subject to the foregoing provisions of this section . . ." This refers back to section 2(1) which incorporates Community law into our system. Section 2(4) could therefore be said to give supremacy to Community law. But it can also be held to mean no more than it creates a presumption that, if there is a conflict between Community and domestic law, any ambiguity in that domestic law will be resolved to give effect to our Community obligations.

Initially the English courts took the view that English law and Community law were of equal status and that, by the doctrine of implied repeal, the courts should give effect to whatever represented the latest intention of Parliament (see *e.g. Bulmer (HP) Ltd. v. J. Bollinger SA* (C.A., 1974)). Indeed on many occasions the approach was to avoid the problem altogether by treating section 2(4) simply as a principle of construction. So in *Garland v. B.R. Engineering Co.* (H.L., 1983), an alleged conflict between section 6(4) of the Sex Discrimination Act 1975 and Article 119 of the Treaty and subsequent directives, was resolved by construing the Act widely. (See also the approach in *Duke v. G.E.C. Reliance* (H.L., 1988) and *Pickstone v. Freemans plc* (H.L., 1989).)

Even where the courts indicated that priority should be given to Community law, our courts attempted to uphold the traditional view on sovereignty by arguing that Community law "is not supplanting English law. It is part of our law which overrides any other part which is inconsistent with it" (*per* Lord Denning M.R. in *Macarthys v. Smith* (C.A., 1981)). But where there is clear indication that Parliament did not intend to fulfil its obligations under the Treaty and intentionally and expressly acted inconsistently with it, Lord Denning felt it was the duty of our courts to follow the domestic statutes.

The courts seem finally to have accepted a modification of Dicey's approach in *R. v. The Secretary of State for Transport, ex p. Factortame Ltd.* (H.L., 1990). Following the introduction of fishing quotas by the EC, Britain attempted to protect the interests of its fishermen by enacting the Merchant Shipping Act 1988. This prevented foreign nationals from securing part of the British quota by quota-hopping, for example by registering a company in this country. A number of Spanish fishermen who had been utilising part of the British quota by such methods, challenged the validity of the Merchant Shipping Act on the grounds that it violated their rights under Community Law. A preliminary ruling was requested under Article 177. In the meantime they applied for interim relief. The House of Lords in *Factortame 1* (1989) refused to grant interim relief. (See Chap. 7.) It did, however, recognise that if the European Court ruled in favour of the applicants, the English courts would have to find a remedy and this might mean refusing to apply the provisions of the Merchant Shipping Act. On a further reference (*Factortame No. 2* (1991)) the Court of Justice reiterated the well established principle of Community law that a national court must set aside a domestic law which prevented Community law from having full effect. The matter then came back to the House of Lords in 1990. On this occasion their lordships granted interim relief to prevent the act being enforced on the basis that the applicants had shown a strong prima facie case and the other grounds for granting interim relief had been met.

Thus the House of Lords had suspended the operation of the Merchant Shipping Act, effectively challenging its validity and had accepted that where there was a conflict, Community law would prevail. In the subsequent Scottish case of *Murray v. Rogers* (1992) the Court of Session refused to challenge the validity of the Scottish community charge legislation, saying they had normally no power to consider whether an Act of Parliament was valid but that the position might be different if it had been incompatible with Community law.

Factortame 1 did, however, leave open the question raised by Lord Denning M.R. in *Macarthys* as to whether the British Parliament retained the power to legislate expressly in contravention of British treaty obligations.

(In 1991 the E.C.J. ruled on the substantive application that the Merchant Shipping Act was incompatible with the Treaty.)

---

2. THE EXECUTIVE

THE POWERS AND FUNCTIONS OF THE STATE

The state has three types of function: legislative, judicial and executive. The legislative function is exercised mainly through Parliament which has the power to make laws of general applicability and to grant to other bodies the power to make delegated legislation under authority of an act of parliament. Originally the monarch had the power to make laws by means of royal proclamation. A residue of this is the power to make *orders in council*.

The state also has authority to determine disputes which arise out of the operation of its laws. Such disputes are allocated to courts, tribunals or even to government ministers, who, increasingly, exercise functions of a judicial nature. No clear principles determine the allocation of disputes to these bodies although the greater the element of discretion and the more important the policy considerations, the less likely it is for the courts to take on the new area of responsibility.

The state has various executive functions. It must initiate, formulate and direct general policy. That policy must then be put into operation, monitored and regulated. Responsibility for this is with the government of the country, the main decisions being taken by the Cabinet and put into effect by the various government departments and a range of quasi-autonomous bodies.

The doctrine of separation of powers

In the eighteenth century, Montesquieu argued that there were three entirely separate functions of government: legislative, executive and judicial, and that these three functions should be exercised by entirely separate organs, Parliament, the Executive and the Courts. There should, he argued, be no overlap of personnel or function. Otherwise too much power would be concentrated in the hands of one organ and this would lead to tyranny.

Quite clearly there is no strict separation of powers in this country today. There are overlaps of personnel. The Prime Minister and the Cabinet are drawn from Parliament. The Lord Chancellor is a member of all three organs of government. Although Parliament is the main legislative organ, the courts and the executive both have legislative responsibilities. Government ministers have legislative, executive and judicial functions.

Indeed it is extremely difficult to establish any truly satisfactory system of defining the limits of these functions. Rather they seem to merge. Yet it has proved necessary to attempt this task to determine the appropriate checks and balances in the system. Quite clearly the courts' attitude to intervention to control any abuse of power is affected by the nature of the power being exercised. (See *Re Racal Communications Ltd.* (H.L., 1981) and *Vine v. National Dock Labour Board* (H.L., 1957).)

Prerogative power

The powers of the state must be exercised in accordance with the law by virtue of authority granted by the law. In modern times this authority is generally granted by statute but certain powers, rights and immunities appertaining to the Crown still have their origins in the common law. These, originally exercised by the monarch personally, are known as prerogative powers.

Some prerogatives relate to the legislative functions of government. For example, the administration of overseas territories has been accomplished by means of orders in council issued by virtue of the royal prerogative. An example of a judicial prerogative is the prerogative of mercy. The prerogative gives the state widespread powers regarding the disposition and control of the armed forces, power to take action in an emergency, authority to make treaties and declarations of war and peace, and still remains of some importance in foreign affairs.

The prerogative may be superseded by statute. (See *R. v. Home Secretary, ex p. Fire Brigades Union* (C.A., 1994). Where the statutory provision deals with the same area, the prerogative may be extinguished either expressly or by implication. (See *Att.-Gen. v. De Keyser's Royal Hotel* (H.L., 1920). But c.f. *R. v. Home Secretary, ex p. Northumbria Police Authority* (C.A., 1988)).

In the past the courts have been willing to interfere only to a limited extent in the use of prerogative power. In *Laker Airways v. Department of Trade* (H.C., 1976) the court indicated that while it would determine the existence and the scope of the prerogative power, it would not review the propriety or adequacy of the grounds on which it had been exercised. This followed cases such as *Chandler v. D.P.P.* (H.L., 1964) where the court refused to review the way in which prerogative power was used.

However, in *Council for Civil Service Unions v. Minister for the Civil Service* (H.L., 1984), the House of Lords recognised the possibility of reviewing the exercise of prerogative power on the same grounds as power granted under statutory provisions. (See especially Lord Scarman.) An example of the courts reviewing a prerogative power can be seen in *R. v. Secretary of State for Foreign and Commonwealth Affairs, ex p. Everett* (Q.B., 1989). Not every exercise of the prerogative will be reviewable. It is clear that the courts still regard some areas as non-justiciable, *i.e.* unsuitable for discussion and review by the courts. Examples which have been given include the control of the armed forces and the exercise of the prerogative in foreign affairs. (See also *R. v. Secretary of State for the Home Department, ex p. Cheblak* (C.A., 1991) and *R. v. Secretary of State for Foreign and Commonwealth Affairs, ex parte Rees Mogg* (D.C., 1994).)

THE CABINET AND THE PRIME MINISTER

All major government decisions are taken by the Cabinet, a committee of senior government ministers. It is for the cabinet to determine the policies to be submitted to Parliament, to determine the content and priorities of legislative proposals, and to ensure that the relevant policies are carried out.

By convention all members of the Cabinet are collectively responsible for decisions taken. While the matter is under discussion ministers can air their views but once the matter is decided all members of the Government, whether within the Cabinet or not, must support it. If they are unable to do this then they should resign as Michael Heseltine did during the Westland affair. The force with which this convention is observed has varied with the political climate. Indeed it was formally suspended during the campaign prior to the referendum on continuing membership of the EC.

There are no rules prescribing the size of the Cabinet. It has varied this century from small war time cabinets where the ministers have had no departmental responsibilities, to cabinets consisting of more than 20 ministers representing all the main departments of state. Increasingly the cabinet operates through a network of committees, the result being that ministers may be bound by decisions in which they have had little more than nominal participation. The terms of reference of these committees and their membership were made public for the first time in 1992.

As with the Cabinet itself, the office of Prime Minister is one which is barely recognised in law. This century has seen a steady increase in the powers of the Prime Minister who is now in a very strong position.

(a) As leader of the party in power, he has been chosen by the electorate, has control over the party machinery and can normally rely on the strength of party loyalty to maintain his position. His public profile is higher than that of any other minister.

(b) As chairman of the cabinet, he can to a large extent determine the nature of discussions within cabinet. No votes are customarily taken. Rather, the Prime Minister sums up the sense of the meeting. Matters can be referred to sub-committees and the agenda manipulated to ensure the desired result.

(c) As ultimate head of the civil service, the Prime Minister has certain powers over senior appointments and access to all information. The publication of "Questions of Procedure for Ministers" in 1992, a document of guidance to ministers prepared by the Cabinet Office, illustrates the extent of Prime Ministerial power over ministers.

(d) The Cabinet Office, although technically providing a service for all members of the cabinet, has grown in recent years into the Prime Minister's special source of assistance and information. This greatly strengthens the Prime Minister's ability to argue against proposals put forward by departmental ministers who are forced to rely almost entirely on the briefs prepared for them by their departmental civil servants.

(e) The Prime Minister is the source of much patronage. He appoints and dismisses government ministers and has at his disposal a wide selection of public appointments, honours, etc.

It is, however, wrong to think of the Prime Minister as having absolute power. However dominant, he must keep the support of his party　both inside and outside Parliament. Ultimately his strength will depend on his personality, but as Rodney Brazier points out, when affairs go badly his authority will wane and if luck deserts him he may well be finished. The removal of Prime Minister Thatcher in 1990 following her failure to win conclusively in the first ballot of the leadership election, emphasises the Prime Minister's ultimate dependence on continued party support. This is further evidenced by the 1995 leadership election in the Conservative Party.

Government Departments

The various tasks undertaken by Central Government are executed by Government Departments such as the Treasury, the Home Office, the Department of the Environment. The organisation and responsibilities of these vary from time to time. At the head of each is a government minister, normally assisted by one or more junior ministers. Each minister will have a Parliamentary Private Secretary. By convention these will all be members of Parliament although not necessarily from the House of Commons. There is no legal limit on the number of ministers but there is a limit on the number who can sit and vote in the Commons (House of Commons Disqualification Act 1975, s.2(1)), presently 95 and a limit to the number of ministerial salaries which can be paid (Ministerial and other Salaries Act 1975).

The departments are staffed by professional civil servants, each one headed by a Permanent Secretary. Civil servants must serve whatever government is in power even if they are not in sympathy with that government's views. To ensure this impartiality there are stringent restrictions on the degree of political involvement permitted to civil servants.

Government Agencies

The 1988 report, "Improving Management in Government, the Next Steps", led to the establishment of a number of government agencies. The aim was to rationalise the bureaucracy and to introduce a more management-oriented system. These new agencies now carry out many of the functions formerly performed by the various government departments. For example much of the work of the Department of Social Security (DSS) is carried out by the Contributions Agency, the Benefits Agency and the Child Support Agency. The framework document which establishes their scope, emphasises that they remain part of the DSS and act on behalf of the Secretary of State. Operational matters are made the responsibility of the chief executive of each agency which is run by a management board. The Permanent Secretary to the Department carries out a monitoring function on behalf of the Secretary of State. The permanent secretary remains the principal advisor on policy matters.

Ministerial responsibility

By convention, ministers are responsible to Parliament for the conduct of their departments (*Carltona v. Commissioner of Works* (C.A., 1943)). In practical terms this may mean:

(a) Ministers may be legally responsible for the acts and omissions of their department.

(b) Ministers are accountable to Parliament which has the right to question the minister on any aspect of the work of the department, even regarding events prior to his taking office.

(c) The degree of personal responsibility depends on the circumstances. Herbert Morrison once argued that ministers were responsible for every stamp stuck on every envelope and that if faults occurred within a department, the minister was at fault in that he had failed to lay down adequate procedures and systems of control. The modern tendency is that the minister is not required to shelter a civil servant who has acted improperly, particularly if he has disobeyed instructions or failed to follow established procedures.

Conversely, in 1991, the Home Secretary, Kenneth Baker, was able to shelter behind his legal advisers when he failed to order compliance with a judicial order requiring the return of a Zairean teacher to this country following his application for judicial review, arguing in the House that he had followed legal advice. Legally, however, he was technically responsible, the court holding that he had acted in contempt of court (*M. v. Home Office* (H.L., 1991)).

Ministers who feel personally to blame, will normally resign, as for example Lord Carrington as Foreign Secretary following the Argentinian invasion of the Falkland Islands and ministers such as John Profumo and David Mellor who were involved in personal scandals. Otherwise, if a minister is criticised, no clear pattern emerges as to whether he will resign. Largely this is a political question depending on a number of factors such as the government's strength and the need to relieve pressure on it. (See the resignation of Leon Brittan during the Westland affair, and the pressures on William Waldegrave arising out of the Scott investigation.)

THE AVAILABILITY OF OFFICIAL INFORMATION

The traditional attitude of government has been that official information should remain secret unless the government chooses to make it available. This has sometimes been justified on security grounds but often the argument has been that disclosure is not in the public interest, that "secrecy is at all times the condition in which the best men make the best decisions."

The series of legal actions initiated by the Government to suppress publication of the memoirs of a former intelligence agent, Peter Wright, indicates the lengths to which the Government will go to ensure confidentiality. In *A.G. v. Guardian Newspapers (No. 2)* (H.L., 1988) it was accepted that the Crown had a right to attempt to restrain disclosure of confidential information relating to the operation of the security services but that they must establish that the disclosure was in some way damaging to the public interest. In view of the widespread publicity given to Peter Wright's book "Spycatcher" it was felt that such damage could not now be established and the injunction against publication was discharged.

Cabinet discussions

The courts have protected the secrecy of cabinet discussions by granting injunctions and by refusing applications for discovery of documents. In *Att.-Gen. v. Jonathan Cape Ltd.* (H.C., 1976) the court held that it had the power to restrain publication of material relating to such discussions although the power was not then exercised. In *Conway v. Rimmer* (H.L., 1968) the need for secrecy was justified because: (a) it ensured full and frank discussion within the cabinet; (b) it helped to preserve the convention of collective responsibility; (c) it protected governments from ill-formed or captious criticism.

This is less than convincing and the suspicion exists that the true reason for secrecy is to protect governments against criticism.

It is interesting to contrast the attitude of the British courts with that of the American Supreme Court where, in the *Pentagon*

Papers Case, an order to restrain publication of accounts of high level discussion about policy in Vietnam, was refused.

The Public Records Acts 1958–67

These protect cabinet documents and other government papers for 30 years, unless the Government chooses to make them available. The period can be extended if continued secrecy is deemed to be in the public interest.

An informal attempt to provide more official information was begun in 1977 when following the "Croham Directive" there was encouragement to government departments to make available background material relating to policy studies and reports. These, it said, should be made available as a matter of course unless a positive decision was taken to suppress the material. However, the effect of this was negligible and as it proved to be an expensive exercise, it was an early casualty of government spending cuts.

In 1981, the Wilson Committee recommended that more papers should be released within the 30-year period and that as few as possible should be withheld beyond 30 years. A 1982 White Paper again recommended greater disclosure suggesting that if the document itself could not be issued, material should be disclosed to enable the public to know the type of information which was being withheld. The White Paper accepted that it was sometimes necessary for whole categories of documents to remain secret but felt that the existence of such categories should be reviewed every 20 years. In May 1992, the Foreign Office announced it would review all secret documents withheld for more than 30 years to see which could be released. A 1993 White Paper on Open Government approved greater openness and a Code of Practice on access to Government Information has been introduced. The Ombudsman has investigated several complaints of breaches of this Code and his reports have led to information being released.

The Official Secrets Acts 1911–89

The overwhelming climate of secrecy has long been encouraged and supported by the Official Secrets Act 1911–20 which have been used not simply to prevent disclosure of security information but to prevent the disclosure of all information which governments have chosen not to disclose whether or not there were any national security implications.

The whole emphasis of the first Act in 1889 was on espionage and treason. The aim of the 1911 Act was to strengthen the law against spying. Section 1 covers all forms of spying making it an offence if any person, for purposes prejudicial to the interests of the state:

(a) approaches, inspects ... enters any prohibited place; or
(b) makes any sketch, plan, model or note which ... might be useful to the enemy; or
(c) obtains or communicates to any other person any information ... calculated or intended to be, or which might be useful to the enemy.

In *Chandler v. D.P.P.* (H.L., 1964) members of a group supporting nuclear disarmament were convicted under section 1 following an incident where they entered an R.A.F. base and attempted to obstruct its use. This sabotage was held to fall within the conduct prohibited by section 1. The House of Lords held that the question whether the conduct was prejudicial to the interests of the state was for the court and not for the jury.

Section 2 of the 1920 Act provides that communicating with a foreign agent is evidence of obtaining or attempting to obtain information calculated or intended to be useful to an enemy contrary to section 1 of the Act.

But section 2 of the 1911 Act went far beyond spying, making it an offence to disclose or receive official information. This was not confined to security information but encompassed any information which was not in the interests of the state to disclose. The courts made it very clear that they equated the interests of the state with the interests of the government then in power. (See McCowan J. in *R. v. Ponting* (H.C., 1985).)

This offered the temptation to government to use section 2 to protect itself against potentially damaging disclosures. For example in the "whistleblower" trials of Sarah Tisdall and Clive Ponting no matters of national security seemed to arise. Their disclosures were, however, likely to cause serious political embarrassment to the Government.

The Official Secrets Act 1989, which repealed s.2 of the 1911 Act, is designed to protect more limited classes of official information. Section 1(1) makes it an offence for any member or former member of the security and intelligence services to disclose information relating to, or in support of, these services.

In the case of disclosure of information on defence, international relations, crime, information resulting from unauthorised disclosures or entrusted in confidence by a crown servant, sections 2–6 make disclosure an offence if made without lawful authority and causing damage to the public interest. This is subject to the defence that the accused did not know the nature of the information or realise that its disclosure would be damaging.

While narrowing the old section 2, the Act is unlikely to give protection to a "whistleblower" who felt that the public should be told certain information as there is no specific public interest defence.

The new act clearly falls far short of the demand for freedom of information legislation with a presumption that all official information is in the public domain except where there are clearly defined reasons for restricting disclosure and where there is adequate monitoring to ensure that civil servants and politicians are committed to implementing the principles behind the legislation.

Secrecy can be damaging in that:

(a) the sources of power and influence are obscured;
(b) public servants are not properly accountable;
(c) public participation is seriously hampered;
(d) justice is not often seen to be done;
(e) inefficiency and error are made more likely.

The 1989 Act merely nibbles at the edges. Full scale reform of official secrets legislation is still very much a topic of current debate.

The "D" notice system

This system of self censorship is followed by the media in security matters. Much journalistic material is obtained from official sources "off the record." Because of the width of our official secrets legislation and the effect of laws on breach of confidence and contempt, the use of such information may constitute a breach of the law. Editors require some guidance as to whether action is likely to follow a particular disclosure.

This informal guidance is given by the Defence, Press and Broadcasting Committee which is composed of representatives of government, the armed forces and media. It issues "D" notices advising that those matters listed should not be published as they are required to remain secret for security reasons. Categories of information presently covered include information about nuclear weapons, the British Intelligence Services and the country's readiness for war. Editors can submit individual stories to the committee for guidance. It should be noted that any clearance is purely informal and does not give any immunity from prosecution. There have been occasions where, despite clearance being given by the Committee, the Government has sought an injunction restraining publication. Conversely, publication in breach of a "D" notice is not, of itself, a criminal offence although the likelihood is that it will fall within the ambit of the legislation.

PUBLIC INTEREST IMMUNITY

In the course of a civil action, one party may wish to inspect documents in the possession of the other side. To obtain these it is possible to ask the court to order discovery. An important restriction to this right is the "privilege" granted to the Crown and other public bodies to oppose discovery on the ground that publication is not in the public interest.

The extent of this immunity was stated most widely in *Duncan v. Cammel Laird* (H.L., 1942), where a claim by the Admiralty that documents relating to the construction of a submarine should not be disclosed, was upheld. The House of Lords said that the Crown could claim immunity:

(a) where the *contents* of the document were such that objection could be made in the national interest to their disclosure;

(b) where the documents, although themselves harmless, fell within a *class* of documents which should always be withheld.

Their lordships said that in matters of the public interest, government ministers and not the courts, were the best judge. Accordingly it felt that the minister's affidavit opposing discovery must be accepted as final and conclusive.

This decision enabled the Crown to prohibit, as a matter of course, the disclosure of a wide range of information such as correspondence with government departments, medical records and accident reports, on the ground that disclosure might set a precedent and lead to potentially harmful documents being disclosed in the future. As the courts were unwilling to look behind the minister's affidavit, there was a clear risk that the minister might misuse his power to ensure secrecy for no better reason than administrative convenience. Although there was a voluntary curtailment of the use of this privilege in 1956, the position was severely criticised by the Court of Appeal in three cases in 1965.

The House of Lords reconsidered the question in *Conway v. Rimmer* (1968). Conway, a probationary police officer, was dismissed from the police force and subsequently brought an action for malicious prosecution against a superior officer. He applied for discovery of certain internal police reports. The Home Secretary opposed discovery, alleging that production would not be in the public interest as the reports fell within a class of documents that should always be protected. The House of Lords decided that the affidavit was not conclusive and that, where appropriate, it had the power to inspect the documents in private and decide whether to accept the claim.

It said that in reaching its decision, it had to balance two competing factors:

(a) The public interest that requires the evidence to remain secret. This could be as a result of considerations of national security; to protect the identity of informants; (*e.g. Lonrho v. Shell Petroleum* (H.L., 1980)); to preserve the secrecy of a class of documents (See the arguments above justifying secrecy for cabinet documents; the protection given to documents relating to police discipline in *Halford v. Sharples* (C.A., 1992) and police reports to the C.P.S. in *O'Sullivan v M.P.C.* (H.C., 1995).

(b) The interests of justice which must ensure that all relevant evidence is available to the court. (See *Re HIV Haemophiliac Litigation* (C.A., 1990).)

An additional factor to be taken into account was added by the case of *Air Canada v. Secretary of State (No. 2)* (H.L., 1983), namely the applicant's need for the documents. The applicant must establish that they would be useful in his case.

Following *Conway v. Rimmer*, the courts have on a number of occasions ordered disclosure against the wishes of the Crown. (For example in *Norwich Pharmacal Co. v. Commissioners of Customs and Excise* (H.L., 1974) and *Burmah Oil v. Bank of England* (H.L., 1979).) None of these have involved security considerations although they have tended to assume that the right to overrule the claim of immunity exists in all cases. Nevertheless there is considerable reluctance to question the minister's judgment unless there is a suggestion of bad faith or error on the part of the minister.

In *Thorburn v. Hermon [Channel 4, third party]* (D.C., 1992), Otton J. said that where the Crown opposed discovery to safeguard national security, the courts were in no position to judge whether this was necessary. Information about the work of the security services formed a "class" of information which ought not, in the public interest to be disclosed.

Conway v. Rimmer retained the possibility of "class" claims. There is now a reluctance to accept these and consider each case on its own facts (*R. v. Chief Constable for the West Midlands, ex p. Wiley* (H.L., 1994).

3. PARLIAMENT

THE COMPOSITION OF PARLIAMENT

Parliament consists of three elements:

    (a)   The Monarch.
    (b)   The House of Lords.
    (c)   The House of Commons.

The House of Lords
The Lords Temporal.

    (a)   Hereditary Peers and Peeresses in their own right of the United Kingdom including:
        (i) Holders of titles created in the peerage of England before Union with Scotland in 1707.
        (ii) Holders of titles created in the peerage of Great Britain.
        (iii) All Scottish Peers of the Realm (Peerage Act 1963, s.4).
    (b)   Life Peers appointed under the Life Peerages Act 1958.
    (c)   Lords of Appeal in Ordinary (The Law Lords).

The Lords Spiritual.

    26 Bishops of the Church of England, *viz*: Archbishops of Canterbury and York, the Bishops of London, Durham and Winchester and 21 other Bishops in order of seniority of appointment. They sit only so long as they continue to hold episcopal office.

Disqualification for membership of House of Lords:

    (a)   Aliens.
    (b)   Persons under 21.
    (c)   Undischarged bankrupts.
    (d)   Persons convicted of Treason—until sentence completed or pardon granted—Forfeiture Act 1870.
    (e)   Members expelled by the House unless pardoned.

The House of Commons
There are 650 M.P.s elected on a constituency basis by those entitled to vote by virtue of the Representation of the People Act 1983. Boundary Commission proposals will take the total number of seats in the Commons to 659 after the next general election. All Commonwealth citizens and citizens of the Republic of Ireland are entitled to vote if they are 18, are resident in a parliamentary constituency on the qualifying date, and are not subject to any legal incapacity and appear in the appropriate register of electors. The

presiding officer must decide, when a person tries to vote, if he is suffering from mental illness, is subnormal or intoxicated and so lacks the capacity to understand what he is doing. Convicted criminals in penal institutions are disqualified as are persons convicted of certain corrupt or illegal practices at elections. Elections are conducted by virtue of the "first past the post system," that is the candidate with the largest number of votes in a constituency is returned.

Disqualification for membership of the House of Commons:

(a) Aliens. (*Note*—citizens of the Republic of Ireland are not barred.)
(b) Persons under 21.
(c) Persons of "unsound mind"—Mental Health Act 1983, s.141.
(d) Peers and peeresses in their own right unless there has been a disclaimer under the Peerage Act 1963.
(e) Clergy ordained in the Church of England and Ireland, Ministers of the Church of Scotland and Roman Catholic Priests.
(f) Bankrupts until discharged—Insolvency Act 1986, s.427.
(g) Persons guilty of corrupt or illegal practices at elections. The extent of the disqualification depends on the precise offence—Representation of the People Act 1983, Pt. III.
(h) Persons guilty of treason—until sentence completed or pardon granted.
(i) A person convicted of an offence and sentenced to a term of imprisonment for more than one year—Representation of the People Act 1981. This covers imprisonment in the United Kingdom or the Republic of Ireland.
(j) Those disqualified under the House of Commons Disqualification Act 1975 as holding "an office or place of profit under the Crown." (See updated Schedule, 1990.)

This includes:

(i) Most major judicial offices (but not magistrates).
(ii) Civil servants, members of the armed forces and the police.
(iii) Membership of any legislature outside the Commonwealth. Euro M.P.s are not, however, disqualified.
(iv) Members of various boards, administrative bodies, chairmen of many public authorities.
(v) Under section 4 of the Act, the holders of certain specified offices are disqualified, for example the Steward of the Chiltern Hundreds.

An M.P. who wishes to "resign" his seat must apply for one of the above offices of profit and thereby disqualify himself from sitting.

THE WORK OF PARLIAMENT

The passage of legislation

Origins of legislation

At the beginning of each Parliamentary session, the Monarch opens Parliament with a speech from the throne which outlines the Government's main proposals for the session. The programme will have been carefully considered by the Cabinet which decides on a timetable for the introduction of legislation. The details of this task are entrusted to the Future Legislation Committee of the Cabinet which has to cope with a flood of requests from the various Departments of State who all wish to have their proposals included.

The preparation of legislation is often a lengthy process. The content and policy of the Bill must be approved by the appropriate Cabinet committee and then by the full Cabinet. Reform may sometimes be preceded by Green or White Papers allowing pre-legislative consultation in Parliament. Consultation will also take place with various interest groups. By the end of this pre-legislative stage the main content of the Bill is effectively settled although further negotiations between the various interested parties continue throughout the passage through Parliament.

Responsibility for drafting the Bill is with the Parliamentary Draftsmen, officially known as Parliamentary Counsel to the Treasury. Their draft is scrutinised by the Legislation Committee of the Cabinet. The Lord Chancellor's Office and the Law Officers are also likely to examine the Bill to consider such matters as the proper legal wording and the practicalities of implementation.

Procedure for the passing of a Public Bill introduced by the Government into the House of Commons

1. First Reading. A purely formal stage.

The title of the Bill is read out, an order is made for the Bill to be published and a date fixed for the second reading.

2. Second Reading.

The principles of the Bill are discussed on the floor of the House. The Bill is voted on.

3. Committee Stage.

A detailed clause by clause analysis of the Bill by a standing committee of between 16–50 M.P.s. Detailed amendments are considered.

4. Report Stage.

The Bill is reported back to the whole House as amended. Further amendments, usually government sponsored, can be made at this stage.

5. Third Reading.

Once again the whole House considers the principles behind the legislation. Only verbal amendments can be made and any debate must be supported by at least six members.

Once a Bill has passed its Commons' stage it goes up to the House of Lords where the same process is repeated, except that the Committee stage is taken on the floor of the House. If the Bill is amended in the House of Lords, these amendments must be considered by the Commons. Often these amendments are tabled by the Government and so there is no problem in ensuring that the Commons will approve them. If, however, the amendments are rejected by the Commons, the Lords must decide whether to persist with these. If no agreement is reached before the end of the Session, the Bill will fail. The Government must then decide whether to reintroduce the measure in the following session and invoke the provisions of the Parliament Acts 1911–49.

Once the Bill is passed by both Houses it receives the Royal Assent. This is purely formal.

Variations on this procedure

1. Bills may start life in either House. The Government must try to arrange its business to ensure that the Commons does not have all its work at the beginning of the session and the House of Lords has all its work at the end. Generally less controversial Bills, *e.g.* technical legal Bills are selected to start life in the Lords, high profile political Bills in the Commons. As the House of Commons has sole responsibility for financial matters, it has to carry the burden of the work on financial Bills.

2. Some Bills have their Second Reading Stage in Committee. This is on the motion of a minister but can be prevented if 20 members object. This procedure was introduced in an attempt to save time on the floor of the House and is used for unopposed and non controversial legislation. If the Second Reading is in Committee, the Report Stage will also be in Committee.

3. Some Bills have their committee stage on the floor of the House in the Commons. This procedure can be used for:

(a)　non-controversial Bills where the committee stage would be purely formal;
(b)　Bills of major constitutional importance where all members wish to be involved at every stage;
(c)　Bills passed in an emergency;
(d)　major clauses of Finance Bills.

In these cases Committee and Report Stages will be combined.

4. Bills relating to Scotland alone may be referred to the Scottish Grand Committee unless ten members object.

Effectiveness of parliamentary scrutiny of legislation

It has been argued that the present procedure for the passage of legislation does not provide effective scrutiny, that Parliament simply legitimises that which the Government has decreed. The following factors might indicate that scrutiny is ineffective.

1. The Government has a majority in the Commons and can normally force its measures through relying on such factors as the "whip system' and party loyalty.

2. The Government has control over the Parliamentary time-table and can curtail discussion and bring matters to a vote by the use of various procedural devices such as the "closure." Even in Committee there is no guarantee that every clause will be examined in detail. If a voluntary timetable cannot be agreed then the Government can "guillotine" proceedings.

3. Legislation has increased in volume and complexity over the years. M.P.s may lack the necessary expertise to scrutinise it effectively and may lack the necessary independent information.

4. There is a basic conflict between the need for technical scrutiny of legislation and the political need to oppose the legislation, to make it unworkable rather than improve it. As has been pointed out "the purpose of many opposition amendments is not to make the Bill more generally acceptable but to make the Government less generally acceptable."

5. The power of the House of Lords to amend legislation is limited by the Parliament Acts 1911–49.

(a)　There is no effective power to delay or veto a *money Bill*. This is a Bill certified by the Speaker as containing only provisions relating to the imposition, repeal or regulation of taxation, the imposition or variation of charges on the consolidated fund, etc., supply, the appropriation, receipt, custody, issue or audit of accounts of public money, the raising or guarantee of any loan or the repayment thereof, or subordinate matters incidental to any of the above topics. The Speaker's certificate is conclusive.

(b) In the case of other public Bills (excluding a Bill to extend the life of Parliament) the House of Lords has no power of veto, only a power of delay. If a Bill is passed by the Commons in two successive sessions having been rejected by the Lords, it can be presented for the Royal Assent provided that one year has elapsed between the date of its second reading in the Commons in the first session and the date of its passing by the Commons in the second session. A rare example of the Parliament Acts being invoked occurred during the passage of the War Crimes Act 1991.

Yet Bills are considerably amended during their passage through Parliament. New clauses may be added. Concessions will be made. Parliamentary scrutiny is still important:

(a) It ensures the measure is publicised allowing opinion outside Parliament to make itself felt.

(b) The Government may be able to ignore the opposition but it cannot afford to ignore its own supporters. Back-bench revolts are not unknown, *e.g.* the Shops Bill in 1986, and many government sponsored amendments represent concessions made by Government to its own supporters. Opposition by the Government's own supporters in the House of Lords led to significant alterations to the Police and Magistrates Courts Act 1994 with respect to the composition and appointment of police authorities.

(c) The establishment of Departmental Select Committees has increased the flow of independent information to M.P.s and increased specialist knowledge amongst back-benchers enabling them to scrutinise legislation more effectively.

(d) Party ties are less strong in committee and defeats do occur for the Government. It may then be a difficult political task to reverse these defeats on the floor of the House.

(e) If the House of Lords exercises its power of delay it ensures maximum publicity for the measure in question. Amendments are sometimes accepted by the Government against its better judgment to prevent disruption of the Parliamentary timetable.

It had been said in the past that there was a convention that the House of Lords would not pass amendments calculated to alter the kernel of a Bill approved by the Commons, but in recent years amendments have gone much further than altering the fine details of the Bill. Although it has been traditionally assumed that Labour Governments are more susceptible to defeat in the Lords than Conservative administrations, Brazier concludes that the Lords have been surprisingly even-handed in dealing out legislative defeats.

Private Members' Bills

Backbenchers can introduce Bills in the following circumstances:

1. By being successful in the Ballot.
2. Under the 10-Minute Rule.
3. Under Standing Order 58.

On average 10–12 Private Members' Bills become law each session. These are mainly Ballot Bills.

Ballot Bills. At a ballot at the beginning of each session, 20 names are drawn out of the hat by the Deputy Speaker. Those members, in order, have an opportunity to introduce their Bills before the House. Ten Fridays are set aside in each session for the passage of such Bills although the Government can give extra time to measures it supports to ensure success.

The subjects chosen are wide ranging. A number of important social reforms have resulted from Ballot Bills such as abortion and divorce law reform. The only restriction is that the main purpose of the Bill must not be public expenditure. If some incidental expenditure is involved, the member must persuade a minister to move a financial resolution.

The procedure is identical to that of any other public Bill. Responsibility for drafting the Bill is borne by the Member although drafting assistance is given to any member whose Bill appears to have a chance of becoming law.

Not all Ballot Bills will be successful. As well as shortage of time, the Bill can be defeated on a vote or it can be talked out. It may be impossible to force a division as the support of 100 M.P.s is needed for the closure. It may also be difficult to maintain a quorum (40).

10-Minute-Rule Bills. Under Standing Order 19 on Tuesdays and Wednesdays after Question Time, one member, selected by the Speaker on a first come, first served basis, has ten minutes in which to outline his proposal for legislation. One speech in reply is permitted and the question is then put. It is extremely unlikely that legislation will result from this. Indeed the member will not have a draft Bill. The main purpose of this procedure is not to initiate legislation but to generate publicity for a particular issue or to test the water to see if there is support for legislation in the future. Even if a "Bill" succeeds at this stage, there is no further time allocated for the remaining stages and so, unless the Government gives up some of its time, the Bill will not proceed further.

A report by the Select Committee on Procedure criticised the abuse of this process for publicity purposes and recommended that the text of any Bill proposed should be first lodged with the Public Bill Office. No action has been taken on this.

Standing Order 58. Under Standing Order 58 a member may present a Bill without obtaining leave from the House. This allows a member to take advantage of any gap in the Parliamentary time-table (these are rare) and present a measure. Only fairly simple, non-controversial Bills are likely to succeed by this method.

Delegated legislation

Not all legislation is made directly by Parliament. Government ministers, local authorities and other public bodies have been given the power by statute to make subordinate legislation. This may be in the form of statutory instruments and orders, byelaws, regulations and orders in council.

The most important type of delegated legislation made by a minister is a statutory instrument. This is defined and regulated by The Statutory Instruments Act 1946.

Delegated legislation made by a minister acting under statutory authority which does not fall within this definition, is known as a statutory order. There is no more precise definition as it is simply a residual category. Statutory orders are not regulated by the 1946 Act.

Uses of delegated legislation

Delegated legislation is used mainly to add detail to primary legislation which may lay down the general principles although matters of considerable importance are sometimes dealt with in this way.

The use of delegated legislation saves Parliamentary time:

(a) Parliament can concentrate on the principles and ignore the details which can be worked out elsewhere.
(b) If the law requires updating this can be done without taking up time on the floor of the House.

It can also be said that the use of delegated legislation is desirable:

(a) it allows a certain flexibility in the law. It enables the minister, for example, to bring sections of an act into effect as and when required. It allows for regional variations. It even allows for a degree of experimentation in that the delegated legislation can be used to alter provisions in the parent act.
(b) it facilitates full consultation with experts. Consideration of

detailed, technical, legislation in the contentious atmosphere of the floor of the House cannot be desirable.

But it does have its dangers, particularly when used to effect changes of substance. Then it can be argued that too much power is being concentrated in the hands of the minister. The procedure is much less public than that for the passage of Acts of Parliament. Clearly it is essential that, to prevent abuse, there is adequate control.

Control over delegated legislation

The enabling Act. The law-making power which Parliament intends to delegate should be expressed in clear and unambiguous language. The grant of wide discretionary powers makes it much more difficult to control the exercise of these powers by means of the doctrine of *ultra vires*. The enabling Act also determines the form in which the power is to be exercised. Greater control will be achieved by providing that the power is to be exercised by way of statutory instrument. It will then be regulated by the Statutory Instruments Act 1946 and will, if laid before Parliament, be subject to the scrutiny of the Joint Committee on Delegated Legislation.

Laying before Parliament. The enabling Act can provide that the instrument is to be laid before either or both Houses of Parliament. Various types of laying procedures are used:

(a) Greatest control is achieved by making the order subject to an affirmative resolution. This means the instrument will not come into effect until approved by Parliament in accordance with the laying requirement. The Government must then make time for the resolution to be discussed although, as the Government has a majority and can normally force its measures through, it is unusual for such resolutions to be unsuccessful.

(b) Where an order is subject to a negative resolution it must be laid before Parliament (usually for 40 days) during which time a member can move a prayer to annul it. The order may come into effect as soon as it is signed by the relevant minister. If annulled it will simply cease being law. Attempts to annul such orders are rarely successful. Prayers must be moved at the end of the day's business, an unpopular time. Time for discussion is severely limited. The Government will normally have a majority and even if defeated, can reintroduce the measure and pressurise its supporters to defeat the motion. The order cannot be amended, simply withdrawn.

(c) Other forms of laying procedure are laying for information only and laying in draft.

Section 4 of the Statutory Instruments Act 1946 says that where a statutory instrument is required to be laid before Parliament then it *shall* be laid before the instrument comes into operation. This is subject to the proviso that where it is essential that an instrument comes into effect immediately, it can be brought into effect before it is laid, but that the Speaker and/or Lord Chancellor should be informed of this and the reason for it. In *R. v. Sheer Metalcraft* (H.C., 1954) Streatfield J. said that a statutory instrument was complete "when made and laid." Together with section 4 this suggests that laying is a mandatory procedural requirement. However *R. v. Secretary of State for the Environment, ex p. Leicester C.C.* (H.C., 1985) said that where an order had to be laid before Parliament, laying before the House of Commons was sufficient as there had been substantial compliance with the procedural requirements.

Publication. One difficulty in ensuring adequate scrutiny of delegated legislation is that not all delegated legislation need be published. In the case of statutory orders, any specific requirements as to publication must be stated in the enabling act. Statutory instruments are regulated by section 2 of the Act and must be sent to the Queen's Printer, numbered and put on sale. Some statutory instruments are exempt from this requirement by virtue of the Statutory Instruments Regulations 1947. This exempts instruments of a local or temporary nature, bulky Schedules and instruments which, in the opinion of the minister, it is not in the public interest to publish. Failure to comply with section 2 does not render the order invalid. (*Sheer Metalcraft, supra.*)

It should, however, be noted, that section 3(2) of the Act provides a limited defence in the case of a person charged with an offence under an unpublished statutory instrument. In any proceedings it shall be a defence for the accused to prove that, at the date of the alleged contravention, the instrument had not been issued by Her Majesty's Stationery Office. It is then up to the Minister to defeat the defence by proving that he had taken reasonable steps to bring the purport of the instrument to the notice of the public or of persons likely to be affected by it, or of the person charged. It is unlikely that this defence will be available in the case of every unpublished statutory instrument. The wording of section 3(2) appears to confine it to instruments which should have been published but, in fact, were not. This would exclude instruments exempted by the Minister under the 1947 regulations and other types of delegated legislation. How strictly the section is to be construed remains in some doubt.

Scrutiny by Parliamentary Committee. The Joint Committee on Statutory Instruments, which comprises seven members from each House plus a chairman drawn from the Opposition benches in the Commons, can examine all general statutory instruments and all other statutory orders subject to the affirmative procedure or special procedure orders. It is not concerned with the merits of the instruments but rather with whether the special attention of the House should be drawn to the legislation in that it:

(a) imposes a tax or fee on the public or a charge on the public revenue;

(b) is made pursuant of an enactment containing specific provisions excluding it from challenge in the courts;

(c) purports to have retrospective effect when there is no express authority in the enabling statute;

(d) has been unduly delayed in publication or laying before Parliament;

(e) has come into operation before being laid before Parliament and there has been unjustifiable delay in informing the Speaker;

(f) is of doubtful *vires* or makes some unusual or unexpected use of the powers conferred by the enabling statute;

(g) calls for any special reason of form or content, for elucidation;

(h) is defective in its drafting.

The Committee can consider only a fraction of the instruments laid before Parliament. Even when the Committee draws special attention to an instrument, no special Parliamentary notice need be taken. Indeed, by the time the Committee has reported, the instrument in question may have been dealt with.

Scrutiny by the Courts. The courts may be asked to consider whether delegated legislation is *ultra vires* the enabling act. (See Chap. 6.) In interpreting the width of the power to make delegated legislation, the courts will apply certain presumptions, *e.g.* (a) that there is no power to impose a tax unless stated expressly (*Att.-Gen. v. Wilts United Dairies* (C.A., 1921)); and (b) that there is no power to oust the citizen's right of access to the courts (*Chester v. Bateson* (H.C., 1920)).

Parliamentary scrutiny of the Executive

Not since the nineteenth century can it be said that Parliament has made policy directly. This function has long since passed to the Cabinet. Parliament can still influence policy making, acting during the formulation by way of various interest groups and committees and by general expression of opinion on the floor of the House. Sometimes it is given the opportunity to express its views more formally in the course of debates following the publication of Green and White Papers.

Its impact is limited by the strength of the Government which generally can control its own supporters and rely on its majority in the Commons. It is, today, simply one of many interest groups attempting to influence the decision-making process.

Parliament has, however, attempted to cling tenaciously to its role in the scrutiny of the implementation of that policy. After all, constitutionally, ministers are answerable to Parliament for the conduct of their Departments. There are a number of opportunities in the Parliamentary year to examine the Government's record.

Debates

The Opposition parties have 20 days in each session in which they can select the topic for debate. Formerly this time was known as "Supply Days" and was used to discuss the grant of supply to the Crown but it has long ceased to be confined to discussion of government spending and is instead used to criticise all aspects of government policy. The Government itself provides time to debate such matters as the armed services and the EU, topics traditionally debated during supply days.

Emergency Debates are allowed at the discretion of the Speaker under Standing Order 20 if he considers that an application relates to "a specific and important matter that should have urgent consideration." The application must be supported by 40 members. There is reluctance to allow such debates in view of the considerable disruption caused to the Parliamentary timetable. There are, on average, two a year.

Certain opportunities are given to backbenchers to choose the subject matter for debate. Examples are:

(a) Adjournment Debates—half hour debates at the end of each day's sitting. Members ballot for a right to choose a topic and speak. A government minister will reply.
(b) Ten Fridays and four half days are given for private members' motions.
(c) Adjournment Debates following the passage of the Consolidated Fund and Appropriation Bills.

Apart from Emergency Debates which, because of their rarity will command widespread coverage in the media, such debates have limited value. The outcome is rarely in doubt. The opposition of the Opposition can be taken for granted. More important will be dissent shown during the debates by the Government's own supporters.

Parliamentary questions

Ministers are questioned in the House on a rota basis for 45 to 55 minutes on Mondays to Thursdays. The Prime Minister takes the last 15 minutes of question time on Tuesdays and Thursdays. Members can give no more than ten days notice of a question and the questions are listed in the order in which they are tabled.

According to Erskine May the purpose is to obtain information, to press for action. It now appears that question time is used for the following purposes:

(a) To embarrass the Government by raising a sensitive issue.
(b) To publicise a particular matter, either nationally or in the M.P.'s own constituency.
(c) To keep the Minister on his toes, to ensure he is *au fait* with the activities of his Department. This is done by asking an "open question" whose significance is not immediately apparent, and following it up with a supplementary. The Minister may be surprised into revealing more than he intended or reduced to admitting he does not know the answer, or even misleading the House. All these may do considerable damage to his reputation. Such open questions are widely used during questions to the Prime Minister. Parliament is currently considering proposals to restrict their use.
(d) Some questions asked by the Government's own back benchers are "planted" by the Minister to enable him to release information.
(e) Prime Minister's Question time is often used by the Opposition to make political points. It has variously been described as a "bear baiting session" and "a ritual exchange of non information."

Thus question time has limited use in obtaining the factual information necessary to enable M.P.s to scrutinise the activities of the Government. Ministers have warning of questions and need disclose no more information than they think fit and are obliged only to answer those matters which fall within their particular areas of responsibility. Thus as a formal method of scrutiny it has little value.

Written answers to questions. Questions not dealt with on the floor of the House are answered in writing by the Minister and the answers published in Hansard. In addition, questions may be put down for written answer. Such questions are designed:

(a) to obtain factual information;
(b) to take up matters on behalf of constituents.

Although these may produce useful information, Ministers are skilled in revealing no more than is necessary.

One basic defect in these methods of scrutiny is that M.P.s must know the right questions to ask. As Government becomes more complex, it becomes increasingly difficult for M.P.s to have sufficient specialist knowledge to identify the key areas for investigation. Specialist knowledge, developed through membership of parliamentary committees, has proved invaluable here.

Parliamentary Select Committees

A more effective method of scrutiny than can be employed on the floor of the House is scrutiny by committees of M.P.s. 14 departmental select committees were established in 1979 to shadow the various departments of state such as Industry, Education and Environment. Three Committees, Foreign Affairs, Home Affairs and Treasury and Civil Service have appointed sub-committees.

Membership. Committees normally consist of 11 M.P.s, their membership reflecting party balance in the House. The chairmanships are shared between Conservative and Labour, the Government retaining some of the most sensitive, *e.g.* Defence, for itself. The committee members are appointed by the Committee of Selection. There is keen competition among backbenchers for places on the most prestigious committees and some complaints that the Committee of Selection tends to appoint mainstream party members to the exclusion of formidable establishment critics. After the 1992 election over 200 M.P.s applied for 96 committee places.

Terms of Reference. "To provide continuous and systematic scrutiny of the activities of the public service and to base that scrutiny on the subject areas within the responsibility of the individual Government Departments."

Specifically the committees have the following functions:

(a) To examine departmental estimates, to examine the policy objectives underlying these and consider whether the expenditure incurred would achieve these objectives in an economical manner. (The committees are supplied with proof copies of the estimates.)
(b) To examine all aspects of administration and policy relating to the department.
(c) To undertake special studies of areas of importance within the ambit of the department.
(d) To have a limited function in the examination of delegated legislation and European Secondary Legislation.

Powers. The committees are empowered to take evidence from

ministers, civil servants and outside experts and to call for the
necessary papers and records. The committee must, however, rely
on Parliament to enforce these powers and this depends on the
wishes of the Government of the day. The Select Committee on
Defence investigating the "Westland Affair" wished to question
civil service press officers and the Prime Minister's Press Secretary
but the Government's refusal to allow them to testify effectively
emasculated the committee. The committee accepted a compromise
and took evidence from Sir Robert Armstrong and another
senior civil servant. When the former Parliamentary Under Secretary
of State for Health (Mrs Edwina Currie) had refused to give
evidence to the Select Committee on Agriculture, the committee
resolved to table a motion in the Commons forcing her attendance.
She agreed to appear but her answers contributed little
information.

Assessment. The committees have produced a considerable
amount of valuable information which must assist M.P.s in their
general task of scrutiny. The subjects studied have been wide ranging.
They have not shied away from sensitive areas. In general it
is felt that investigations into specific problems have been more
valuable than wide ranging background investigations.

The reports have attracted considerable publicity although only
a tiny proportion of the reports have been debated in the House.
Clearly where a committee can issue a quick and reasoned comment
on a topical subject it has the greatest impact. Committees
are beginning to time their reports to correspond with appropriate
business, such as legislation or a planned debate and this ensures
greater coverage of their report. A major problem has been the
delay before the government department in question produces any
response to the report. The Committee on Procedure recommended
a maximum of two months but this was not accepted.
While some departments have attempted to adhere to this informally,
there have been too many exceptions. M.P.s themselves appear
enthusiastic and keen to participate. There have been no problems
in staffing the committees and the membership has remained relatively
static. This has enabled M.P.s to build up considerable
expertise in their chosen fields. The Committees have all appointed
specialist advisors. There is some evidence that committee members
feel themselves less fettered by party ties in committee than
on the floor of the House although there has been a tendency for
party loyalty to reassert itself if the report is debated.

Yet the Committees cannot force ministers and civil servants to divulge information. The government has made it clear that it believes a civil servant's responsibility is to his minister, not to Parliament. This has led one M.P. to describe civil servants giving evidence to a committee as being "paralysed with caution".

Most commentators agree, for example, that the investigation by the Select Committee on Trade and Industry into the supply of a "supergun" to Iraq in breach of an embargo on arms sales, failed to uncover the truth. (Select Committee Report 1992.)

Thus the new system may be an improvement but there is little evidence to support the view that the new committees exercise any real systematic control over the activities of government.

Control over financial matters

Constitutionally, Parliament has control over taxation and expenditure, although once again decisions are made by the Government. Those taxes imposed annually must be authorised by the Finance Act. Authority for levying taxation in the interim period is given by the Provisional Collection of Taxes Act 1968, a resolution of the House of Commons being insufficient authority (*Bowles v. The Bank of England* (H.C., 1913)).

Every year as part of the planning process leading to the Budget the government carries out its public expenditure survey (PES), reviewing its spending plans for the next two financial years and planning for Year 3. It sets an annual ceiling for most public spending. Departments then bid for a share. These bids are fitted in to the amount available by a process of negotiation. Much of the work on this is done by the Chief Secretary to the Treasury and a cabinet committee known by the initials EDX and chaired by the Chancellor.

Parliament's contribution to this process is confined to a debate on the Chancellor's statement and formal approval of government spending (*e.g.* by passing the Annual Appropriation Act which authorises payments out of the consolidated fund).

There is little detailed Parliamentary control. Debates on the floor of the House are rarely concerned with matters of detail. The various departmental select committees looking at the estimates and the Public Accounts Committee looking at the accounts of what has been spent, can only scratch the surface. There is no Parliamentary control over Government borrowing.

The Comptroller and Auditor General, appointed by the Crown on a resolution of the House of Commons by virtue of section 1(1) of the National Audit Act 1983 has two major functions: (a) to ensure that all money paid out of the government accounts has been properly authorised and is properly applied; and (b) to examine the accounts of the various government departments. Under the Audit Act 1983 this is more than a traditional audit. He is entitled to consider whether "objectives have been achieved in the most economical way." This has become known as "value for money" and "efficiency" auditing. He is not, however, entitled to question the merits of the policy itself.

He then reports to the Public Accounts Committee who will follow up a selection of his reports.

The National Audit Office, of which he is head, is also responsible for auditing the accounts of a wide range of bodies dependent on funds from central government such as the National Health Service and the Universities.

PARLIAMENTARY PRIVILEGE

To ensure that Members of Parliament and Parliament as a whole can carry out their functions effectively, they have certain privileges to safeguard them from outside interference.

Privilege of freedom of speech

To ensure an M.P. is free to carry out his Parliamentary duties and speak freely without fear of any legal repercussions, an M.P. has the privilege of free speech.

1. M.P.s have *absolute privilege* with regards to words spoken in the course of Parliamentary proceedings. (The Bill of Rights, Art. 9.) Not only does this protect against actions of defamation but also against any criminal charges. Nor can they be found to be in contempt of court in relation to words spoken in the course of proceedings in Parliament.

In *Church of Scientology v. Johnson Smith* (H.C., 1972) an attempt was made to sue an M.P. claiming that he had slandered the Church of Scientology and its members. In order to succeed, it was necessary to show that the M.P. had spoken with malice. It was attempted to prove this by relying on a speech made by him in Parliament. The court held that these words could not be used as the words were absolutely privileged.

What are proceedings before Parliament?

It clearly covers debates, questions and everything said and done by a member both in committee and on the floor of the House.

But as Erskine May points out, it does not follow that everything which is said and done within the confines of the chamber during a debate or other business forms part of a proceeding in Parliament. It would not, for example, cover a private conversation between two M.P.s. Nor does the geographical location of the speaker give automatic protection: *Rivilin v. Bilainkin* (H.C., 1953). A private conversation is not a proceeding before Parliament.

Difficulties have arisen as to whether letters written to Ministers by M.P.s in the course of their duties are covered by absolute privilege. This question arose in the *Strauss* case in 1958 when an M.P., taking up a matter on behalf of a constituent, made certain allegations against the Electricity Board. The Chairman of the Board immediately issued a writ for libel. Strauss alleged that this was an infringement of his absolute privilege of free speech and as such was a contempt of Parliament.

The matter was referred to the Committee on Privileges which recommended that the matter was covered by absolute privilege but when this was debated by the whole House, it was accepted that writing to a minister was not a proceeding before Parliament. Accordingly the House rejected the committee's recommendations and ruled that the issuing of the libel writ was not a contempt. In fact the writ was then withdrawn.

Parliament is not bound to follow this in the future. Indeed the view has sometimes been expressed that there is a clear advantage in keeping the scope of this privilege indefinite. Despite this there have been various Parliamentary attempts to define the phrase. In Session 1969–70 the Select Committee on Privileges recommended that it should cover:

(a) all things done or written in each House or in Committee for the purpose of business being transacted;

(b) all things done between members and officers, between members, and between members and ministers for the purpose of enabling any of these to carry out their functions.

A possible limitation to this is the suggestion that it would cover only those matters which had been before the House, or at least those coming before the House in the current Parliamentary session.

2. Qualified Privilege. An M.P. may rely on the defence of qualified privilege in regard to words spoken in the course of his duty as an M.P. This means that he is protected against any action of defamation provided he speaks in good faith and without malice (*Beach v. Freeson* (H.C., 1972)), and provided there is a common interest between the parties.

In recent years M.P.s have made use of this privilege to make defamatory allegations. Perhaps the most serious incident was where several M.P.s deliberately identified an officer of the security services who had given evidence in court under the name Colonel B. The court had warned that any attempt to name the officer would be a contempt of court. No action could be taken by the court against the M.P.s.

While Parliament itself can regulate such matters it has shown itself reluctant to do more than call on "the good sense of M.P.s not to abuse their privilege."

In 1995 the High Court halted a libel action by two M.P.'s against the Guardian newspaper on the basis that much of the evidence could not be explored as it related to "proceedings in Parliament". (See also *Rost v. Edwards*, H.C., 1990).

Reports of Parliamentary Proceedings

At common law no protection was given to those reporting speeches made in Parliament. The M.P. was absolutely privileged but the reporter and the publisher could face civil or criminal action (*Stockdale v. Hansard* (H.L., 1839), where libel damages were awarded against Hansard who had printed verbatim an authorised House of Commons Report).

Protection is now given by the Parliamentary Papers Act 1840. Section 1 gives *absolute protection* against any civil or criminal action to anyone publishing papers printed by order of Parliament. This will cover, for example, White Papers and Hansard, the daily journal of the House. If any proceedings based on such papers are initiated, these must be stayed on production of a certificate issued by the Speaker or the Lord Chancellor. Section 2 gives *absolute protection* to any copy of such paper. Section 3 only protects against actions of defamation in that it gives *qualified privilege* to extracts from any reports protected by sections 1 and 2. This means that such extracts are protected provided the defendant can show that they were published in good faith and without malice. (*Dingle v. Associated Newspapers* (H.C., 1960).) Reports of Parliamentary proceedings are protected by the ordinary law of defamation in so far as they are fair and accurate unless the defamed person can prove malice. The basis of this protection is that publication is deemed to be for the benefit of the public. In *Cook v. Alexander* (C.A., 1973) qualified privilege was accorded to a "Parliamentary Sketch" which, although impressionistic and selective, was considered by the court to be sufficiently balanced as to be fair and reasonable. No special protection has been given to the broadcasting of the proceedings of the House, although it seems likely the defence of qualified privilege to actions of defamation will be available.

Privilege of freedom from arrest

M.P.s have no privilege protecting them against an arrest on criminal charges but they are protected against arrest in connection with a civil matter while Parliament is in session and for 40 days before and after. This is of no real practical importance today.

Parliament's right to determine its own composition.

1. The Commons has the right to fill casual vacancies by calling a by-election.

2. The Commons can determine the result of disputed elections. In practice this is now dealt with by an Election Court. (Representation of the People Act 1983, Pt. III.)

3. Parliament has the right to determine whether members are legally disqualified. In the *Wedgwood Benn* case 1961 the House of Commons refused to allow Tony Benn to take his seat although he had been duly elected. He had succeeded to a peerage on the death of his father and was disqualified from sitting in the Commons.

4. The House may expel members whom it considers unfit to serve.

Parliament's right to regulate its own internal proceedings

Parliament is empowered to regulate its own internal proceedings. It may make standing orders to govern its procedures. The courts have always refused to consider whether these procedures have been complied with. *Pickin v. British Rail Board* (H.L., 1974).

The privilege is much wider than procedural matters, covering every aspect of the internal functions of the House. In *R. v. Graham-Campbell, ex p. Herbert* (H.C., 1935) the Court refused to investigate an alleged breach of the licensing laws by the "Kitchen Committee" of the House of Commons.

In *Bradlaugh v. Gossett* (H.C., 1884) Parliament expelled an M.P. who refused to take the oath of allegiance to the Crown under the Parliamentary Oaths Act 1866, on the ground that he was an atheist and the oath would be meaningless. At a by-election he was re-elected and indicated that he was now willing to take the requisite oath. Parliament resolved that he should be prevented, if necessary by force, from taking his seat. It was said that "the House of Commons is not subject to the control of the courts in the administration of that part of statute law which has relevance to its own internal proceedings." The court would not intervene. Following the report of the Nolan Committee, a House of Commons' Select Committee on Standards in Public Life, recommended the appointment of a Parliamentary Commissioner for Standards to investigate allegations of improper behaviour by M.P.'s and the establishment of a Standards Committee which will hold public hearings into alleged breaches.

Parliament's power to punish for contempt

The following have been held to be contempts of Parliament:

1. An attempt to interfere with a Member's freedom of action. In the *N.U.P.E. Case* (H.C. 1976/77) the national conference of N.U.P.E. passed a resolution demanding that the union's executive withdraw union sponsorship from those M.P.s who supported their party's public expenditure cuts. The Committee of Privileges found this to be a contempt but no action was taken when the General Secretary of the Union gave assurances that sanctions would not be imposed on M.P.s. Other attempts to obstruct members in the execution of their duty such as bribery or threats have also constituted contempt.

2. Misconduct in the House or disobedience of the rules of the House, *e.g.* failure to co-operate with a Parliamentary Committee, disruptive behaviour in the House.

3. Misconduct by M.P.s in the House. When John Profumo was found to have lied to the House this was a contempt. (*Profumo's Case 1962/63.*) Corruption, taking bribes, failure to declare a conflict in interests have all constituted contempts. Recent concerns have related to the employment of M.P.'s as consultants and lobbyists and the employment of ex-cabinet ministers in positions where use could be made of their "inside knowledge". (See the Nolan Report.)

4. Publication of materials reflecting on the proceedings of the House and its members. Newspaper articles criticising M.P.s have been held to be a contempt. (*Sunday People Case* (H.C., 1976/67).) Publication of false reports of Parliamentary proceedings and premature disclosure of committee proceedings have both constituted contempt.

Thus contempt is wider than simply breach of any of Parliament's privileges but can consist of any conduct which interferes with the workings of Parliament or is likely to bring Parliament or its members into disrepute. If an M.P. feels that a contempt has occurred, he first complains to the Speaker who considers whether a breach of privilege has prima facie occurred. If so, the House has the opportunity to consider whether the matter should be referred to the Committee of Privileges or the new Standards Committee.

Members can be suspended or expelled for contempt. The House also has the power to admonish or issue a reprimand to those in contempt. Journalists may be barred from the House for a period of time. While the House has the power to imprison for contempt, this was last used in 1880. The House has no power to fine although this has been recommended.

THE ROLE OF THE HOUSE OF LORDS

It has often been argued that the House of Lords should be abolished and that we should have a unicameral system of Government. The House of Lords has been criticised on the following grounds:

1. Its composition. The hereditary nature of the House has been criticised. It is argued that birth is an illogical and inappropriate criterion for membership. It draws on a narrow social class who are not representative of the country as a whole. The introduction of life peerages was partly designed to broaden the base of membership but it can be argued that life peers have not made as large a contribution to the work of the House as had been hoped. Too often it has been used as a reward for political service.

2. It is not elected. It has been argued that it is wrong for such a body to impose even a limited check on the activities of an elected Government.

3. In the past it was criticised for political bias. It was alleged that there was an in-built conservative majority. The introduction of the life peerage system and the fact that peers can apply for leave of absence at the beginning of each session has tended to redress this although those taking the Conservative Whip constitute the largest single grouping. In recent years Conservative administrations have faced greater opposition from the House of Lords than have Labour Governments, partly because there is probably a greater fear of a Labour Government curtailing still further the powers of the Lords should it be faced with opposition from that quarter.

Yet it does perform a number of useful functions.

1. Legislative functions.

(a) A number of Bills, mainly non-controversial, start life in the Lords.
(b) The House does a considerable amount of scrutiny of complex and technical legislation. Many Government amendments are brought in the Lords to save time in the Commons. It is generally accepted that the House has had in recent years, an increased impact. (See,

for example, their input into the Police and Magistrates Court Act 1994.)
(c)   It bears the brunt of the examination of private Bills.
(d)   It does valuable work in the scrutiny of delegated legislation including European secondary legislation.

Not only does this save time in the Commons, it provides another type of less politically charged scrutiny by those who may have a wide range of expertise and experience.

2. Debating function.

The House of Lords provides a useful forum for debating the great issues of the day.

3. Check on government.

It is argued that in view of the impotence of the House of Commons and the flexibility of the British Constitution, it is necessary for there to be some check on the activities of Government. Although limited by the Parliament Acts and the convention of non-involvement in financial matters, the House of Lords is the only such check. The Lords can publicise matters and delay action for long enough to allow public opinion to make itself felt.

Reform of the House of Lords

Composition

(a) An elected chamber. This could be on the basis of multi-member constituencies and some form of proportional representation or on the existing first-past-the-post system. The obvious difficulty of having the same method of election for both Houses is that it would tend to produce a mirror image and devalue the House of Lords as a check. If a different method was employed there would undoubtedly be arguments as to which House better represented the wishes of the people.

(b) An appointed chamber. The second chamber could be appointed either by the Prime Minister as under the present system for the appointment of life peers or by various interest groups who would be entitled to nominate representatives.

Concern has been expressed about extending further the Prime Minister's powers of patronage. It could also be questioned whether a system of specialised representatives is desirable in that it may not produce a group of people willing to take an overall view of the question.

An attempt at reform was instigated in 1968 where a Bill providing for a two-tier system of voting and non-voting peers was introduced. The voting members were to be peers of first creation.

Hereditary peers were to be allowed to retain their seats, speak but not vote. It was suggested that the number of voting peers should be about 230, that the Government of the day should always have the largest number of peers but not an absolute majority. The balance of power should be held by cross-benchers. The Bill did not become law.

Functions

It has been suggested that the delaying power of the House of Lords should be reduced still further.

Conversely it has been argued that if the composition of the House of Lords was altered, giving it more credibility, then its powers should correspondingly be increased. Only then would persons of the right calibre be attracted to serve in it. In particular it has been argued that any body which has no power over financial matters is impotent as a check on the activities of government and that a new "upper chamber" should have some control over financial matters.

4. THE POLICE AND THE PUBLIC

THE INVESTIGATION OF OFFENCES

The police are entrusted with the power to investigate offences, yet, just because a person comes under suspicion of being involved in criminal activity, does not mean that he loses all rights to the freedom of his person. The law has to strike a balance between preserving and safeguarding the rights of individuals and giving the police the necessary powers to carry out these tasks effectively.

The police have the right to ask anyone questions in the course of their duties but, although there may be a moral duty to help the police, there is no legal duty.

(a) There is no obligation to answer questions. (*Rice v. Connolly* (H.L., 1966).) A person should not be forced to incriminate himself. It should be noted that in certain circumstances a failure to answer questions may have evidential consequences. Changes implemented by sections 34–39 of the Criminal Justice and Public Order Act 1994 mean that a suspect is still able to choose to remain silent, but that the court is allowed in certain circumstances to draw an adverse inference from the suspect's silence. Silence on its own will not prove guilt and remaining silent will not of itself, be sufficient evidence of guilt. The prosecution will always be required to produce other evidence.

Thus under section 34, where a suspect is being questioned under caution or is being charged with an offence, and fails to mention a fact which he subsequently relies on in his defence, the court may be allowed to draw an adverse influence from the suspect's silence, if it considers it to have been reasonable for the accused to have mentioned the fact when questioned or charged. Under section 36 a similar inference may be drawn from a failure to provide an explanation where objects, substances or marks are found on a suspect or in the place the suspect was at the time of the offence.

Before such an inference can be drawn, the requirements of section 36(b), (c) and (d) must be satisfied.

(b) Failure to answer police questions does not, by itself, amount to obstruction of the police in the execution of their duty;

(c) If a person is voluntarily helping the police, that person is entitled to terminate the interview and leave at any time. If the police wish to detain him they must place him under arrest. Section 29 of the Police and Criminal Evidence Act 1984 (PACE) provides that he should be informed at once that he is under arrest if a decision is taken to prevent him leaving at will.

Power to stop and search

Under section 1 of PACE the police can stop and search:

(a) any person or vehicle;
(b) anything which is in or on a vehicle,

for stolen or prohibited articles or articles with blades or points as defined in section 139 of the Criminal Justice Act 1984, and may detain a person or vehicle in order to conduct such a search.

A prohibited article includes:

(a) an offensive weapon;
(b) an article made for, or intended to be used for, burglary, theft, theft of a motor vehicle, obtaining property by deception.

The officer must have reasonable grounds for stop and search (s.1(3)). Whether such grounds exist will depend on the circumstances of each case but there must be some objective basis for it. A Code of Practice on Stop and Search says that an officer will need to consider the nature of the article suspected of being carried in the context of other factors such as the time, place and behaviour of the person concerned or those with him. Reasonable suspicion may exist, for example, when information has been received such as a description of an article being carried.

Reasonable suspicion can never be supported on the basis of personal factors alone. For example a person's colour, age, hairstyle or manner of dress or the fact that he is known to have a previous conviction for possession of an unlawful article, cannot be used alone or in combination with each other as the sole basis on which to search that person. Nor may it be founded on the basis of stereotyped images of certain persons or groups as more likely to be committing offences.

The extent of the search

The Code envisages a minimal interference with a person's liberty, perhaps lasting a minute or so. Searches are restricted to superficial examination of outer clothing. The thoroughness and extent of the search depends on what is suspected of being carried. So, for example, if the suspicion relates to an article slipped into a pocket, the power of search will relate only to that pocket. If a fuller search is deemed necessary, it must be done in a suitable place by an officer of the same sex and unless the suspect consents to accompany the officer, he must first be arrested.

It should be noted that in certain circumstances a failure to answer questions may have evidential consequences. Changes implemented by sections 34–39 of the Criminal Justice and Public Order Act 1994 mean that a suspect is still able to choose to remain silent, but that the court is allowed in certain circumstances to draw an adverse inference from the suspect's silence. Silence on its own will not prove guilt and remaining silent will not of itself, be sufficient evidence of guilt. The prosecution will always be required to produce other evidence.

Thus under section 34, where a suspect is being questioned under caution or is being charged with an offence, and fails to mention a fact which he subsequently relies on in his defence, the court may be allowed to draw an adverse inference from the suspect's silence, if it considers it to have been reasonable for the accused to have mentioned the fact when questioned or charged. Under section 36 a similar inference may be drawn from a failure to provide an explanation where objects, substances or marks are found on a suspect or in the place the suspect was at the time of the offence.

Before such an inference can be drawn the requirements of section 36(b), (c) and (d) must be satisfied.

Location of search

The power can be exercised in any place to which the public has access whether on payment or not, excluding dwelling houses or other private premises such as private clubs. It covers streets, common areas of flats, such as stairs and walkways, gardens easily accessible from the street, pub car parks, etc.

Other powers

PACE does not encompass all existing stop and search powers. Other powers are given by such Acts as the Firearms Act 1968 (persons, vehicles in any public place can be searched for firearms) and the Misuse of Drugs Act 1971 (permits the police to stop and search for controlled drugs anywhere). Under section 60 of the Criminal Justice and Public Order Act 1994, where it is reasonably believed that incidents involving serious violence may take place in a locality and it is expedient to use the powers given under the Act to prevent their occurrence an officer of the rank of Superintendent or above may authorise special stop and search powers (See Ch.5.) A uniformed officer may then search any person for offensive weapons. There is no need for the officer to have any level of suspicion against the person being searched.

In general the safeguards detailed below apply to these Acts. In practice a large number of searches proceed with the consent of the suspect in which case the provisions of PACE do not apply. It should however be noted that juveniles and the mentally handicapped will always be protected by the provisions of PACE as they cannot give consent to a voluntary search.

Safeguards

While it is recognised that such powers may be necessary in that they lead to a number of arrests, it must also be noted that random and discriminatory stops may be counter-productive as they may have a detrimental effect on relations between police and public. Young people and ethnic minorities have repeatedly complained about police harassment.

Section 2 accordingly requires the following safeguards:

(a)   The officer must identify himself (s.2(3)(a));
(b)   He must take reasonable steps to explain what he is looking for and the basis of his suspicion (s.2(3)(b));
(c)   He must normally make a record of the search there and then unless this is impracticable. This should cover the ethnic group, identity of the suspect, object, grounds of search, place and time, date and results (s.3). This record should be made available to the suspect on request and is designed to facilitate any complaints of unjustifiable action by the police;
(d)   If an unattended vehicle has been searched, a note should be left recording this fact and indicating the officer responsible (s.2(6)).

The effectiveness of such safeguards must, to a large extent, depend on the institutional pressure on the police to keep adequate records.

If the officer is satisfied with the suspect's response he need not proceed with the search. In that case no record need be kept.

Arrest

This is a fundamental step in the criminal process designed to ensure the person is available to answer charges before a court. It must be remembered that it is not the only way in which a person can be brought before a court. In the case of less serious offences a person can be summonsed to appear.

The justification for the arrest

Arrest under warrant. Under section 1 of the Magistrates' Court Act 1980, a warrant for arrest may be issued by a magistrate on sworn information by the police. It must identify the suspect and the offence on which it is founded.

Summary power of arrest. In the following circumstances the police have the power to arrest without a warrant.

Arrestable offences

Section 24 provides for a power of summary arrest in respect of arrestable offences as defined in that section.

An *arrestable offence* is:

(1) an offence for which the sentence is fixed by law (murder, treason);
(2) an offence for which a person of 21 or over may be sentenced on first conviction to imprisonment for a term of five years (this covers common law and statutory offences);
(3) those offences listed in section 24(2), *e.g.* Theft Act 1968 (ss.12(1) and 25(1)). These do not meet the sentencing requirement but are nevertheless deemed to be arrestable offences.

Conspiring or attempting to commit such offences, inciting, aiding, abetting, counselling or procuring the commission of such offences are also arrestable offences.

Some offences under section 24(2) already attracted a power of summary arrest under individual statutes. The effect of making them arrestable is that it gives the police certain powers of entry and search under section 17 and 18 while investigating the offences in question.

Section 26 repealed a number of existing statutory provisions which allowed summary arrest. Those retained are listed in Schedule 2 of the Act. These preserved powers of arrest include offences under the Immigration Act 1971 and various public order offences, *e.g.* The Criminal Justice and Public Order Act 1994.

The combined effect of these provisions is to give a power of summary arrest in the case of all the more serious offences and many of the most commonly committed offences, *e.g.* murder, manslaughter, the major offences against the person, offences under the Criminal Damage Act and almost all the Theft Act offences.

The police and the citizen may arrest:

(a) Anyone who is in the act of committing an arrestable offence.
(b) Anyone whom he has reasonable grounds for suspecting to be committing such an offence.
(c) Anyone who has committed an arrestable offence or he has reasonable grounds for suspecting has committed an arrestable offence.

The police officer has additional powers of arrest.

(a) He can arrest where he has reasonable grounds for suspecting that an arrestable offence has been committed and he has reasonable grounds for suspecting the person to be guilty of the offence.
(b) He has a preventative power in that he can arrest anyone who is about to, or he has reasonable grounds to suspect is about to, commit an arrestable offence.

Where service of a summons is impracticable

Under section 25 the police have a power of summary arrest in the case of non-arrestable offences, but only where service of a summons appears to the officer to be impracticable or inappropriate because any of the *general arrest conditions* noted below apply. These are:

(a) That the officer cannot discover the suspect's name or believes he has given a false name. (*Nicholas v. D.P.P.* (H.C., 1987).)
(b) That there is no satisfactory address for serving the summons.
(c) That the constable has reasonable grounds for believing that arrest is necessary to prevent the relevant person:
    (i) causing physical harm to himself or another;
    (ii) suffering physical injury;
    (iii) causing loss or damage to property;
    (iv) committing an offence against public decency;
    (v) causing an unlawful obstruction of the highway.
(d) That the constable has reasonable grounds for believing that an arrest is necessary, *e.g.* to protect a child.

To prevent a breach of the peace

At common law the police have long had the power to effect an arrest to prevent a breach of the peace. (*R. v. Howell* (C.A., 1981.)

Formalities of Arrest

The Act requires the person arrested to be informed that he is under arrest as soon as this is practicable. This must be done even if the fact that he is under arrest is obvious (s.28(1) and (2)).

The suspect must also be told of the ground of the arrest at the time or as soon as is practicable thereafter (s.28(3) and *D.P.P. v. Hawkins* (H.C., 1988)). In *Edwards v. D.P.P.* (H.C., 1993) the fact that the police officer gave a wrong reason for the arrest, rendered the arrest invalid.

Section 28 enacts in statutory form the rule laid down in *Christie v. Leachinsky* (H.L., 1947) where Lord Simon said that the suspect was entitled to know on what charge or on suspicion of what crime he was seized. If the citizen is not so informed the police may be liable for false imprisonment unless, of course, the suspect makes this impossible by his conduct. (*Lewis v. Chief Constable of South Wales* (C.A., 1990.) Lord Simon stressed that technical or precise language need not be used (see *Abbassy v. Newman* (C.A., 1989)). Section 28 varies the decision in *Leachinsky* in that Lord Simon said that if the facts were obvious, if, for example the suspect has been caught red handed, it was not necessary to inform him why he had been arrested. Section 28(4) now says that the person must be told the reason for the arrest even if the facts are obvious. (*Nicholas v. D.P.P.* (H.C., 1987).)

Arrest elsewhere than at a police station

When a person is arrested away from a police station, section 30 says that he should be taken to a police station as soon as practicable unless the investigation requires his presence elsewhere. This must normally be a designated station, that is one which has a custody officer and has the necessary facilitates to cope with those detained following arrest. (But, see *Vince and Another v. Chief Constable of Dorset* (C.A., 1992.) He need not be taken to a designated police station if it is not anticipated he will be detained for more than six hours or where the arresting officer is without help.

Search on arrest

Section 32 regulates searches where an arrest is made away from a police station. A constable has a right to search for a weapon if he has reasonable grounds for believing that the suspect might present a danger to himself or others, for example because he was acting violently or was drunk or suicidal. The suspect may also be searched for anything he could use to effect his escape and for evidence relating to any offence if there are reasonable grounds for suspecting that the items are in the suspect's possession.

Such a search must be relatively cursory. If a person is searched in public he cannot be required to remove anything other than his coat, jacket or gloves.

Following an arrest the police may search the premises where the suspect was immediately prior to or at the time of the arrest for evidence relating to that offence (s.32(2)(*b*)). (*R. v. Beckford* (C.A., 1991).) If he has been arrested for an arrestable offence, there may also be a power to search his home under section 18.

Section 54 requires the custody officer to ascertain what property a detained person has with him. He is responsible for its safekeeping. To that end he is entitled to search him. Cash and items of value are kept for safekeeping. The detained person can retain his clothing and personal effects unless the custody officer considers he may use them to cause harm to himself or others, effect an escape, damage property or interfere with evidence.

Section 54(6)A gives an additional power of search at any time in order to ascertain whether he has with him any items which could be used for the purposes specified above.

Apart from the clothing and personal effects mentioned above, anything else can be seized. Intimate and Strip searches must be conducted in accordance with Annexe A to Code C.

QUESTIONING IN POLICE CUSTODY

The opportunity to question suspects in custody is clearly of crucial importance to the police. The suspect, however, is in a very vulnerable situation. The Royal Commission on Criminal Justice (The Runciman Commission) emphasised that a fundamental balance must be struck between the public interest in bringing offenders to justice and the protection of the rights and liberties of suspects. The recognition in PACE of the power to detain suspects after arrest, but before charge is balanced by attempts to give some protection to the suspect. These arise from the introduction of maximum time limits for detention, periodic review of the need for such detention, the statutory rights of access to a solicitor and a Code of Practice on Detention and Questioning. The Custody Officer has a pivotal role in ensuring these rules are properly observed. These, together with the introduction of the Crown Prosecution Service and the requirement that suspects' statements be tape recorded, balance the increased powers given to the police to enable them to investigate crime more effectively.

Para 11 of Code C defines an interview as the questioning of a person regarding his involvement or suspected involvement in a criminal offence which, under the Code, must be carried out under caution. This reflects the decision in *R. v. Cox* (C.A., 1993).

The Custody Officer

The Custody Officer is responsible for safeguarding the rights of suspects at the police station. Section 36(5) stresses his independence allowing only minimal involvement at an earlier stage of the investigation.

His main duties are:

(a) To determine if the suspect's detention is valid. If not he should be released with or without bail (s.34(1)).

(b) To determine whether there is sufficient evidence to charge him (s.37(1) and para. 17 Code). He must not delay charging to allow questioning to continue.

(c) If the suspect is not charged the custody officer may be required to release him. The presumption is that the suspect will be released with or without bail, but it can be rebutted if the custody officer has reasonable grounds for believing that detention without charge is necessary to secure or preserve evidence relating to the offence for which the suspect has been arrested, or to obtain such evidence by questioning him (s.37(2)).

(d) To keep the custody record which records the history of the detention (s.39(1)(*b*) and para. 12 of Code). The record is available to the suspect on request for 12 months.

(e) To ensure that the suspect is treated in accordance with the provisions of the Act and the Code of Practice (see below).

(f) To itemise the suspect's property (see above).

(g) To inform the suspect of the reason for the detention, of his right to legal advice and his right to have a person informed that he is in custody and his right to consult the Codes of Practice.

The right to legal advice and to have a person informed

A person who is in police detention is entitled to consult a solicitor privately at any time (s.58). The suspect must be told of this right both orally and in writing and will be asked to sign the custody record saying that this has been done. The availability of legal aid must be drawn to his attention and a poster outlining the right to legal advice must be displayed prominently in the charging area. The Code of Practice emphasises that no attempt should be made to dissuade a person from obtaining legal advice.

The suspect also has the right to have one person informed that he is in custody. That person may be a friend, a relative or other

person who is likely to take an interest in his welfare (s.56, para.
5 Code).

These are not absolute rights. In the case of serious arrestable
offences the rights can be postponed for up to 36 hours on the
authority of an officer of at least the rank of superintendent if that
officer has reasonable grounds for believing that the exercise of
either right would:

(a) lead to interference with evidence connected with a serious arrest-
     able offence;
(b) lead to interference with or physical injury to other persons;
(c) "tip-off" other persons suspected of a serious arrestable offence;
(d) hinder the recovery of property.

It is not sufficient reason for postponement of these rights that
a solicitor might advise his client to remain silent (*R. v. Neil McIvor*
(Cr.C., 1987)). There must be a belief that the solicitor would
commit the criminal offence of alerting other suspects or be hood-
winked into doing so inadvertently or unwittingly. In *R. v. Samuel*
(C.A., 1988), the court felt that either belief could only rarely be
genuinely held by a police officer. If such a belief could be supported, the suspect should be offered access to another solicitor.

Serious arrestable offences—definition—section 116

1. Some arrestable offences are so serious that they are always
serious arrestable offences. These are listed in Schedule 5 of the Act and
include murder, manslaughter, rape, treason, kidnapping, causing
explosions likely to endanger life or property and hijacking.

2. Any other arrestable offence may be *serious* if its commission
has led to or is likely to lead to:

(a) serious harm to the security of the state or public order;
(b) serious interference with the administration of justice or with the
     investigation of offences;
(c) death;
(d) serious injury;
(e) substantial financial gain or serious financial loss.
     (Loss is serious if it is serious for the person who suffers it.)

This last ground has given rise to some difficulty in interpretation. Clearly the intention was that run of the mill thefts should
not be serious arrestable offences. In *R. v. Neil McIvor* the court
held that the police had wrongly considered the theft of 28 dogs
owned by a hunt as a serious arrestable offence as the loss to the
members of the hunt could not be considered a serious financial
loss. In *R. v. Eric Smith* (Cr.C., 1987), it was felt that the police had
wrongly considered a theft totalling £1,000 from a large company a

serious arrestable offence. It would not be considered a serious loss by the company and the financial gain to the robbers was not necessarily substantial. However in *R. v. Samuel* the theft of £300 from a building society was considered a serious arrestable offence, both because of the use of a sawn-off shot gun in the raid and also because of the accused's intention to cause serious financial loss to the building society.

The exercise of the right

The Code says that consultation with a solicitor can be in person, in writing or by telephone. Note the use of the Duty Solicitor Scheme and the provision of free legal advice under the Green Form Scheme to facilitate this. About one third of suspects exercise this right. Much of this advice has been given by clerks rather than solicitors and the quality of the advice given has been questioned. In 1994 the Law Society and the Legal Aid Board initiated a training package "Police Station Skills for Legal Advisers" and an accreditation scheme, in an attempt to improve matters. The Code of Practice C says that non-solicitors must either be trainee solicitors or accredited.

Even where there is an absolute right to legal advice, the suspect can be questioned before that advice is given if he consents, or where, to wait, would cause unreasonable delay or hindrance.

Solicitors may be present during the suspect's interview but the Code says that they may be asked to leave if their conduct prevents the investigating officer properly questioning the suspect. Such an exclusion might entail the solicitor being reported to the Law Society.

Where a relative or friend of a person in custody inquires as to his whereabouts, that person should normally be told unless the detainee objects or unless any of the factors, noted above, justifying delay, apply. The Code provides additional safeguards for juveniles, mentally handicapped persons, the deaf and those who cannot speak or understand English.

The interview

It is the responsibility of the Custody Officer to ensure that detainees are treated in accordance with the Act and the Codes of Practice (s.39(1)). An important provision is therefore that, after arrest, a suspect should not normally be questioned except at the station unless delay would lead to interference with evidence etc. Questioning should normally take place in the interview room and should be tape-recorded. Paras. C3.4 and C15.2A have been inserted to reduce the scope of exchanges between police and suspect at the custody desk and when the detention is subsequently reviewed.

Under paragraph 12 of the Code, the Custody Officer has the power to decide whether the suspect can be interviewed by another officer. In the case of a dispute between the Custody Officer and investigating officer (who may often outrank him), section 39(6) provides that the matter should be referred to an officer of the rank of superintendent or above. The Code requires that there be an adequate record of the interview, that the suspect is given refreshments and allowed periods of rest during extended questioning. Questioning must not be oppressive. The notes of guidance to the Code stress that the purpose of any interview is not necessarily to obtain an admission but to obtain from the suspect his explanation of the facts.

As soon as the investigating officer believes that a prosecution should be brought and there is sufficient evidence for it to succeed, questioning should cease.

Review of detention

An important safeguard introduced by the Act is the periodic review of detention to see if such detention is justified in terms of the detention criteria in section 37(2) noted above. The responsibility for the reviews rests with the *review officer* who, under section 40(1)(*b*), must be an officer of at least the rank of inspector and who has not been directly involved in the investigation. Where a person has been arrested and charged, the review officer is the Custody Officer. The first review takes place not later than six hours from the time the detention was authorised. The second review should not be later than nine hours after the first, *i.e.* 15 hours after the detention was authorised. Subsequent reviews should take place every nine hours thereafter.

Limits on period of detention without charge

At 24 hours, a person not yet charged should be released. Further detention can only be authorised in the case of a person who is suspected of having committed a *serious arrestable offence*.

Continued detention

Detention beyond the 24-hour period up to 36 hours can only be authorised by an officer of the rank of superintendent or above. He must be satisfied that:

    (a)   it is a serious arrestable offence;

(b)   the detention conditions apply;

(c)   the investigation is being conducted diligently and expeditiously.

At the 36-hour point the suspect must be charged, released or an application made for a warrant of further detention. *In the matter of an application for a warrant of further detention* (H.C., 1988), the reason given by the police for continuing the detention was that the suspect's release might impede the arrest of further persons. This was not a valid reason under the Act.

Warrants of further detention

Warrants authorising detention beyond 36 hours must be issued by two magistrates (s.43).

They must be satisfied that:

(a)   it is a serious arrestable offence;

(b)   the detention conditions apply;

(c)   the investigation is being conducted diligently and expeditiously.

The warrant can authorise further detention for periods up to 36 hours. Further applications can be made for extensions up to a maximum of 96 hours from the commencement of the detention. At 96 hours, the suspect must be either charged or released.

The detention clock

In calculating the time limits for detention, the starting point is:

(a)   where a person has been arrested outside the police station—
   (i)   the time he arrives at the relevant station; or
   (ii) the time 24 hours after the time of his arrest, whichever is the earlier;

(b)   where a person attends the police station voluntarily and is subsequently arrested there—the time of arrest.

There are special provisions where a person is arrested in another part of the country or abroad.

Applications to a magistrate should, if possible, be made during normal sittings and, in any event, not between 9p.m. and 10a.m. Section 43(5) gives a six-hour leeway at the 36 hour point in that an application for a warrant of further detention can be made up to 42 hours from the commencement of the detention clock, in a situation where the 36 hour period runs out at a time when it is not possible for a magistrate's court to sit. If, however, it was reasonable for the police to make the application in time, the magistrates must dismiss any application made after the 36 hour point. (See *R. v. Slough JJ., ex p. Stirling* (H.C., 1987).)

The suspect or his solicitor is entitled to make representations to the reviewing officer as to why he should be released. A decision to continue the detention must be recorded in the suspect's custody record with reasons. Where an application for further detention is sought, the suspect must be taken before the magistrates and provided with a copy of the police information against him. He has a right to legal aid and legal representation.

Detention after charge

Section 38(1) allows this:

(1) if necessary to substantiate a name or address;
(2) if the custody officer has reasonable grounds for believing this is necessary:
  (i) for the suspect's own protection;
  (ii) to prevent him from causing physical injury to any other person;
  (iii) to prevent loss or damage to property;
  (iv) to ensure his appearance in court;
  (v) to prevent interference with the administration of justice or with the investigation of offences;
  (vi) juveniles can also be detained in custody if the custody officer believes this to be in the juvenile's own interests.

Otherwise under section 46(2) the accused should be brought before a magistrate as soon as is practicable and in any event, not later than the first sitting after he has been charged. There are detailed provisions for the arranging of special sittings if no regular court is scheduled for the day the accused is charged or the following day.

POWERS OF ENTRY AND SEARCH

Code of Practice B applies to searches of premises for the purpose of an investigation into an alleged offence with the occupier's consent, searches under warrant and searches under ss.17, 18 and 32 of PACE. "Premises" is defined in s.23 of PACE and includes any place and, in particular, any vehicle, vessel, aircraft, tent etc.

Police powers to enter premises come from the following sources:

1. Consent of the occupier.
2. Under statutory power.
3. By virtue of a warrant.

Consent

It is estimated that the largest proportion of searches takes place following the consent of the occupier. In the past it has been alleged that consent was often less than genuine, the person believing that he had no option but to allow the police the right to enter the premises and search. Code of Practice B recognises that consent must mean real consent. The occupier must be told that he can refuse to allow the search and that anything seized may be used in evidence. It provides that if consent is given, it must be in writing.

Statutory powers of entry

(a) To execute a warrant of arrest (s.17(1)(*a*)). To arrest for an arrestable offence (s.17(1)(*b*)). To arrest for offences under the Public Order Act 1986 and the Criminal Law Act 1977 (s.17(1)(*c*)).

(b) To recapture a person who is unlawfully at large and whom the officer is hotly pursuing (s.17(1)(*d*)).

(c) To save life and limb or serious damage to property (s.17(1)(*e*)). The ambit of this appears very wide. While not a new power, it was one not greatly recognised or understood at common law.

(d) Although all other common law powers are abolished, section 17(6) retains the common law power of entry to deal with or prevent a breach of the peace. (*Thomas v. Sawkins* (H.C., 1935).)

(e) Following the arrest of a suspect for an arrestable offence, there is a power under section 18 to search the suspect's premises for evidence relating to the offence, or some connected or similar arrestable offence. If necessary, a police officer can search under this section before taking the suspect to the police station (s.18(5)). Apart from this, such a search must be authorised by an officer of the rank of inspector or above. The phrase "similar" is likely to lead to difficulty.

(f) Section 32(2)(*b*), dealing with the search of anyone arrested for any offence, arrestable or otherwise, allows the police to enter and search the premises where the suspect was at the time of his arrest or immediately before for evidence relating to the offence for which he was arrested. The search must be no more than reasonably required for the purposes of discovering such evidence and there must be reasonable grounds for believing that such evidence will be found. This is an immediate power which must be exercised at the time of the arrest (*R. v. Badham* (1987).)

Although (e) and (f) limit the scope of the search, the effect of section 19 is to allow the police to seize other evidence of other unconnected offences providing this is necessary to prevent evidence being destroyed. (See below.)

(g) There still exist other statutes which authorise the police and/or other officials to enter premises without a warrant *e.g.* Customs and Excise Management Act 1979, s.84(5) which allows entry to a place where there are reasonable grounds to suspect signals or messages being sent to smugglers, sections 11 and 43 of the Planning and Compensation Act 1991, and various statutes giving powers of entry to Electricity and Trading Standards Officers and Firemen. The precise requirements, such as the need for written authority, vary from statute to statute.

Search warrants

There are a number of Acts of Parliament which empower a magistrate on sworn information to issue a warrant to search for such things as stolen goods, forged documents, drugs. These powers are not fully comprehensive, and in the past the police could not, for example, obtain a warrant to search for a murder weapon or evidence of kidnapping.

An additional power was given by section 8 which allows an application to be made to a magistrate for a warrant to search for evidence of a serious arrestable offence.

Before issuing a warrant the magistrate must be satisfied that:

(a) the material is likely to be on the premises.

(b) The material does not comprise matters subject to legal privilege, excluded material or special procedure material.

(c) The material is likely to be of substantial value to the investigation and is likely to be admissible in evidence.

(d) The warrant is necessary, for example, because consent could not be obtained for the search or the element of surprise is necessary. (See s.8(3).)

Few warrants have been issued under section 8.

Items subject to legal privilege

This broadly relates to communications between lawyer and client either in relation to the giving of legal advice or in contemplation of legal proceedings. In *R. v. Snaresbrook Crown Court, ex p. D.P.P.* (D.C., 1988), a legal aid application was held to be subject to legal privilege. Items held with the intention of furthering a criminal purpose are excluded from this category. (See *R. v. Central Criminal Court, ex p. Francis and Francis* (H.C., 1988).) No warrant can be obtained to seize such material. Even if the police "chance" upon it in the course of a legal search, it cannot be taken.

Excluded material

As defined in section 11, this includes journalistic material held in confidence and confidential personal records held by such people as doctors, social workers, etc. No new rights to such material are given by the Act but it does standardise the procedure for applying for a warrant to obtain such material. Applications must be made to a circuit judge, who can issue the warrant by virtue of section 9 and Schedule 1 if he is satisfied that it would have been appropriate to issue a warrant prior to the Act. (This is known as the first set of access conditions.) In *R. v. Central Criminal Court, ex p. Brown* (D.C., 1992), it was held that a judge had no power to issue a warrant to obtain hospital records under section 9 as there had been no right to obtain the materials before PACE.

Special procedure material

Consists of other types of confidential material which does not fall within the definition of excluded material in section 11. It includes material held in confidence which is not classed as "personal records" and certain types of journalistic material not caught by the definition in section 13. Access to special procedure material can only be obtained by virtue of a warrant issued by a circuit judge who can issue such a warrant either where, prior to the Act, there would have been access to such material and the first set of access conditions apply or where the judge has reasonable grounds to believe:

> (i) a serious arrestable offence has been committed;
> (ii) there is special procedure material on the premises;
> (iii) the material is likely to be of substantial value to the investigation;
> (iv) other methods of obtaining the material have been, or are likely to be unsuccessful. (See *R. v. Lewes Crown Court, ex p. Hill* (H.C., 1991).)
> (v) the production of the materials is in the public interest.

(The second set of access conditions.) For examples of application of these, see *R. v. Bristol Crown Court, ex p. Bristol Press and Picture Agency Ltd.* (H.C., 1987) and *Re An Application* under section 9 of the Police and Criminal Evidence Act 1984 (H.C., 1988).

The extent of the search

The Code of Practice on search and seizure emphasises that searches should be carried out with due consideration to the occupants. The police must not ransack premises. The search should be discontinued if it becomes clear that the items sought are not on the premises.

Section 16(8) of the Act says the search may only extend to the purpose for which the warrant is issued. As was said by the Royal Commission, the police should not, on a warrant to search for a stolen grand piano, look under the floorboards or in the water cistern.

Section 8(2) authorises a constable to seize and retain anything for which the search has been authorised. Section 19 permits the constable to seize anything on the premises if he has reasonable grounds for believing either that it has been obtained in consequence of the commission of an offence or that it is evidence in relation to an offence which he is investigating or any other offence. In either case the officer must have reasonable grounds for believing that it is necessary to seize the evidence there and then to prevent it being destroyed. He must be on the premises lawfully, either by virtue of a warrant, under statutory authority or by consent.

Effect of non-compliance with PACE

Evidence obtained in breach of PACE and the Codes may be excluded by virtue of sections 76 and 78. A distinction is drawn between confession and other evidence.

Section 76 Confessions

If it is alleged that a confession has been obtained by oppression or in consequence of anything likely to render it unreliable, the court will not admit it unless the prosecution can prove beyond reasonable doubt that it was not obtained in this way. Oppression may include torture, degrading treatment or the use or threat of violence. It may also arise from "the exercise of authority in a burdensome, harsh or wrongful manner; unjust or cruel treatment." (See *Fulling* (C.A., 1987).)

Bullying or hectoring by police officers might also constitute oppression (*Paris* (C.A., 1982)).

In determining whether anything said or done was likely to render a confession unreliable, the character of the accused will be relevant. So, for example, failure to allow access to a solicitor may constitute oppression in the case of an accused of low intelligence but may not if he is an experienced offender. (See *Alladice* (C.A., 1988) and *Weeks* (C.A., 1994)).

Section 78

The court has a discretion to exclude any evidence, including confessions if it appears to the court, having regard to all the circumstances, that its admission would have such an adverse effect on the fairness of the proceedings that the court ought not to admit it. Failure to comply with provisions of PACE and the accompanying Codes of Practice might be considered to have such an effect. This will be particularly likely if there has been a series of breaches. In *Canale* (C.A., 1990) the court exercised its discretion to exclude evidence where the breaches were seen to be "flagrant, deliberate and cynical." In *Keenan* (C.A., 1990) the court said that, to persuade the court to exercise its discretion to exclude evidence, the breaches must be "significant and substantial." Such breaches as denial of access to a solicitor (*Samuel* (1988)) and failure to tell a suspect of his right to legal advice (*Absolam* (C.A., 1989)) have been viewed as particularly serious. Evidence has also been excluded as a result of failing to keep a proper record of the interview (*Walsh* (C.A., 1989)) and a series of breaches of the Code which, whilst individually were minor, cumulatively were sufficient to cast doubt on the fairness of the proceedings (*Canale, supra*).

POLICE MISCONDUCT

Remedies for unlawful arrest and detention

A basic principle of the rule of law is that any interference with the liberty of the individual must be justified by law. Simply by virtue of his official position no police officer has the right to interfere with a person's liberty unless he can point to legal authority to justify his actions. If a person is detained irregularly or his property or person searched without lawful authority, he has the following remedies:

1. Self Defence. If a person is unlawfully restrained he is entitled to use reasonable force to effect his escape (*Kenlin v. Gardner* (H.C., 1967)). This remedy must be pursued with caution as the amount of force used must be no more than is reasonable in the circumstances. If excessive it may constitute an assault (*Fagan v. M.P.C.* (H.C., 1968)). This may be a very nice judgment to make in a stressful situation.

2. An action of damages may be brought for false imprisonment.

3. An application for a writ of habeas corpus. The system of review of detention introduced under PACE does not affect the system of applications for habeas corpus. An *ex parte* application is made, supported by an affidavit.

4. Action of damages for trespass to the person, or trespass to goods.

5. A person whose chattels have been seized by the police can apply for an order for delivery of the goods and damages under section 3 of the Torts (Interference with Goods) Act 1977.

6. Complaint against the police.

It should be noted that breach of the Codes of Practice does not, of itself, render the police officer liable to any criminal or civil proceedings. The court can, however, take such a breach into account where relevant. Section 67(8) makes police officers liable to disciplinary proceedings for breach of the Code.

Complaints against the police

It was felt by the Royal Commission on Police Powers that criminal prosecution and investigation could only work well if the general public felt confident in the role played by the police. Before 1976 investigation of complaints was essentially an internal police matter. In 1976 the Police Complaints Board was established with limited functions to oversee the disciplining of police officers, who had contravened the Police Disciplinary Code but had not faced criminal charges. They had no powers in relation to criminal actions against the police and no powers of investigation. The present procedure for dealing with complaints was introduced by sections 83–103 of PACE as amended by ss.34–38 of the Police and Magistrates Court Act 1994.

Minor complaints

Minor complaints such as uncivility to a member of the public can be dealt with by a system of informal resolution. The complaint is examined by a Chief Inspector in accordance with the Police (Complaints) Informal Resolution Regulations 1985. An explanation or an apology may resolve the matter. The outcome will be recorded but the finding does not constitute a black mark on the record of the officer involved. If the complaint turns out to be more serious or if agreement cannot be reached on a resolution, it must be referred back for a full investigation.

The system cannot be used unless:

(a) the complainant consents;
(b) the chief officer of police is satisfied that the case would not justify criminal or disciplinary charges being brought.

Note. Conduct which might be classed as criminal is still capable of informal resolution if it is felt that in the circumstances, the officer in question would not be charged.

Supervised complaints

The investigation of the most serious, the most controversial complaints is supervised by the Police Complaints Authority, a body consisting of a chairman appointed by the Queen and not less than 8 other members appointed by the Home Secretary. The Authority is therefore independent of the police. Indeed no one who is, or has been a police officer can be appointed.

The following complaints may be supervised:

1. Mandatory supervision

(a) any complaint alleging conduct leading to death or serious injury.

Section 87(4) defines serious injury as including fracture, damage to internal organs, deep cut, impairment of bodily function;

(b) any complaint alleging the commission of certain other serious offences as listed in the Police Complaints (Mandatory Referrals) Regulations 1985, and including any serious arrestable offence, assault causing actual bodily harm and corruption.

2. Discretionary supervision.

The Complaints Authority can choose or be requested to supervise any other complaint. This may be for example because the matter has political overtones. The PCA may also investigate matters referred to it under section 88 even although no actual complaint has been made. Examples where this power might be used include shooting incidents, deaths in police custody and cases of serious corruption.

The extent of the supervision

1. Control over the officer appointed to investigate.

2. After consultation with the Chief Officer of Police, the power to impose requirements in relation to the conduct of the investigation.

3. Unless the authority is satisfied with the conduct of the investigation, no disciplinary action can be taken. Nor can the DPP normally act.

The Authority has struggled to enhance its supervisory powers. It is now accepted that members of the authority can attend interviews between investigating detectives and police officers under investigation.

At the end of the investigation a copy is sent by the investigating officer to the Chief Officer of Police who will also receive from the Police Complaints Authority a memorandum indicating whether they are satisfied with the investigation.

The result of an unsupervised investigation will also be reported to the Chief Officer of Police. He will then decide whether to send the papers to the DPP or whether to bring disciplinary charges against the officer in question. Under section 90, as amended by the Police and Magistrates Courts Act 1994, the Chief Officer of Police must refer the complaint to the DPP if he believes that a criminal offence has been committed. The Police Complaints Authority will review the outcome of every investigation and has the power to recommend that disciplinary charges be brought and as a last resort order these charges to be brought. Thus even this category of complaint is subject to a measure of supervision.

Note. There is a separate procedure under section 86 for dealing with complaints against senior officers above the rank of chief superintendent. Under this section, the police authority and not the Chief Officer of Police, has the responsibility for ensuring the complaint is investigated.

Comment

1. There has been continued lack of confidence in the system for investigating complaints. The PCA notes that this is particularly the case among members of minority ethnic communities. However rigorously investigations are carried out, the public still see the police investigating themselves. Even the Police Federation has, on occasions expressed its desire for reform. A number of well pub-licised cases have illustrated the difficulties facing investigations of complaints where there is a lack of independent witnesses. As with every professional group there is a tendency to close ranks making evidence gathering difficult. The practical difficulties of estab-lishing an independent investigating body are extensive and there are no current plans to introduce such a body.

2. The reluctance of the DPP to prosecute police officers has attracted criticism. He operates on the basis that there must be a reasonable prospect that a jury is more likely to convict than acquit on the evidence, the 51% rule. The DPP has said that experience has shown that stronger evidence is required than is the norm.

3. The standard of proof which operates at disciplinary hearings is that of the criminal law—beyond reasonable doubt, not the civil standard—on the balance of probabilities. The civil standard regu-lates virtually all other disciplinary bodies apart from the armed forces. The higher criminal standard makes it much more difficult to find there has been a breach of the disciplinary regulations.

A 1993 consultation paper has recommended the development of a two tier system under which cases of unsatisfactory performance would be dealt with internally as a management issue. In cases of serious misconduct there would continue to be a police investi-gation monitored by the PCA in appropriate cases.

No such reform has yet been implemented although the detailed provisions of the Police and Magistrates Court Act mark a move-ment towards a more managerial style of discipline. The PCA con-tinues to argue for a change in the standard of proof in disciplinary cases.

A further concern has been the number of cases where officers facing disciplinary charges have retired or have been discharged on medical grounds before the investigation is completed. The House of Commons Home Affairs Committee has also investigated this and in 1992 new Home Office guidelines were issued.

4. The high rate of withdrawals of complaints (some 40–50 per cent) is worrying. There is concern that improper pressure is sometimes exerted by the police to achieve this.

5. The usage of the informal procedure for dealing with complaints varies considerably from force to force.

6. The system remains very time consuming and bureaucratic. This might discourage its use.

5. PROTEST AND PUBLIC ORDER

The right to demonstrate against unpopular causes has long been considered a bulwark of liberty in any civilised society, enabling groups within that society to attempt to influence public opinion, to express their solidarity, to pressurise government and publicise their cause. Accordingly, the constitutions of many states contain guarantees of the right of peaceful protest.

In the United Kingdom there is no such positive statement of this right, although at common law an assembly or procession is not unlawful *per se*, unless, for example, it causes an obstruction or constitutes a public nuisance.

The public is entitled to use the highway for passage and repassage from one place to another but the extent to which this gives an unrestricted right to hold a moving demonstration on the highway is doubtful. In *Harrison v. Duke of Rutland* (H.C., 1893) it was held that a person who used the highway other than for passage could be sued for trespass. Improper use of the highway might also constitute a nuisance leading to criminal charges, a civil action of damages or an injunction prohibiting the continuation of the improper use. For example, a demonstration outside a firm of estate agents was prohibited, although peaceful (*Hubbard v. Pitt* (H.C., 1976)). In practice, processions appear to have a favoured place providing there is no actual obstruction, that they are peaceful and that police directions are observed (see *Hirst v. Chief Constable of West Yorks* (C.A., 1986)).

Any meeting on private premises must have the consent of the owner. In the past the law has largely dealt with trespassers by way of civil action. The Criminal Justice and Public Order Act 1994 indicates a clear movement towards criminal remedies. See for example the power to remove trespassers under s.61 which strengthens earlier powers and s.68 which is designed to deal with disruptive trespassers, who interfere with lawful activities through disruptive, obstructive or intimidating behaviour by the creation of the offence of "aggravated trespass".

Various bye-laws impose restrictions on where meetings can be held. These may also prohibit the use of loud speakers etc. Meetings in the Royal Parks, Trafalgar Square and near the Houses of Parliament are subject to special rules.

By section 11 of the Public Order Act 1986, anyone organising a march must give the police six days notice otherwise he may commit an offence. When a march is organised at short notice, as much notice as is practicable must be given. The provision is designed to ensure that the policing of the demonstration can be properly planned but the provision has been criticised as unnecessary as most organisers liaised with the police on a voluntary basis. The fear is that the police, whose primary duty is to preserve public order, may have overmuch regard for public order considerations and impose such stringent conditions on holding the march as to make it ineffective as a form of protest. Concern has also been expressed that the provision might also inhibit spontaneous protest.

THE POWERS OF THE POLICE

Conditions
Section 12 of the Act gives the police the power to impose conditions on processions where there is a risk of serious public disorder, to prevent serious damage to property, serious disruption to the life of the community and to prevent intimidation. Such conditions may relate to route, size, timing, etc., of the march. Organising or participating in a march in breach of any such condition constitutes an offence.

Under section 14 the police are given a parallel power to impose conditions on public assemblies.

The power to ban
If the section 12 powers are judged insufficient and there remains a risk of serious public disorder, there is a power, under section 13, to ban processions for any period up to three months. The Chief

Officer of Police may apply to the local authority for a banning order which must be confirmed by the Home Secretary. It is an offence to organise, to participate in or to incite someone to participate in a banned march.

The ban is a blanket ban covering all marches or all marches of a particular class such as political marches. This has caused some concern as peaceful demonstrators may be prevented from marching because of the threat posed by a potentially disruptive counter-demonstration. Yet the suggestion that there should be a power to impose selective bans was rejected, neither police nor judges appearing willing to become involved in such a politically sensitive task, the exercise of which would certainly bring forth accusations of bias.

Section 70 of the 1994 Act introduced a power to ban trespassory assemblies for up to 4 days. These are defined as assemblies which involve at least 20 people, are held on land to which the public has limited or no rights of access and takes place without the permission of the occupier of the land.

Application must be made to the local authority by the chief officer of police on the basis that he believes that an assembly is intended to be held which might result in serious disruption to the life of the community or significant damage to land, building or monuments of historical, architectural or scientific importance. Such a ban may cover an area of not more than a five mile radius.

Other statutory powers

Section 71 of the 1994 Act gives the police a power to prevent persons proceeding to banned trespassory assemblies. Note also the section 60 power to stop and search in anticipation of violence detailed in chapter 4 above.

Powers at common law

At common law, the police have the power to take whatever action is necessary during a demonstration to prevent a breach of the peace. Breach of the peace has been defined as something more than a mere disturbance of the public calm or quiet. In the context of public order, the element of violence deemed essential in *R. v. Howell* (C.A., 1982), in relation to powers of summary arrest, has not always been required. (See *R. v. The Chief Constable of Devon & Cornwall, ex p. C.E.G.B.* (C.A., 1981) where Denning M.R. said that there would be a breach of the peace whenever a person, lawfully carrying out his work, is unlawfully and physically prevented by another from doing it). But in *Percy v. D.P.P.* (D.C., 1994) the court, in determining whether the appellant should have been bound over to keep the peace, followed Howell's case saying that the test was whether there was a real risk of violence or threatened violence occurring.

This power has been used by the police in a variety of ways; to ask demonstrators to leave the scene, even when acting peacefully (*Duncan v. Jones* (H.C., 1936)); to justify the removal of provocative emblems or banners (*Humphries v. Connor* (I.R., 1864)); to direct a procession en route if a breach of the peace is reasonably apprehended (Lord Scarman's Report on the Red Lion Square Disorders). One of the most controversial uses of the power is to prevent demonstrators reaching the scene of the demonstration, a use upheld by the courts in *Moss & Others v. McLachlan* (H.C., 1984). The court held that, providing the police honestly and reasonably believed there was a real risk of a breach of the peace, they were entitled to take reasonable preventative action. What that action consisted of must depend on the imminence or immediacy of the threat to the peace.

In *McConnell v. Chief Constable of the Greater Manchester Police* (C.A., 1990), the Court of Appeal confirmed that a breach of the peace could take place on private premises.

If a meeting is held in private premises it should be noted that the police can insist on entering the premises even against the wishes of the organisers, if they have reasonable grounds to believe a breach of the peace is likely to occur (*Thomas v. Sawkins* (H.C., 1935)), a power confirmed in *McLeod v. M.P.C.* (C.A., 1994).

PUBLIC ORDER OFFENCES

The major public order offences were put on a statutory basis by the Public Order Act 1986:

Riot (s.1)

This is the most serious of the offences in the Act, and is triable only on indictment and attracts a maximum penalty of ten years imprisonment.

> "Where 12 or more persons who are present together use or threaten unlawful violence for a common purpose and the conduct of them (taken together) is such as would cause a person of reasonable firmness present at the scene to fear for his personal safety, each of the persons using unlawful violence for the common purpose is guilty of riot."

In order to obtain a conviction, it must be shown that the accused intends to use violence or is aware that his conduct may be violent.

It should be noted that while 12 persons must be present who are using or threatening violence, only the person charged need be shown to have intended to use the violence. The offence can be committed by aiders and abettors as well as by principals (*R. v Jefferson* (C.A., 1994)). It is unclear the extent to which the 12 need form a cohesive group. Section 8 says that violence means any violent conduct towards persons or property. It is unnecessary to produce a person who fears for his safety. The test is whether a hypothetical bystander of the requisite firmness would suffer such fear.

Violent disorder (s.2)

This is the normal charge for serious outbreaks of public disorder.

> "Where three or more persons who are present together, use or threaten unlawful violence and the conduct of them (taken together) is such as would cause a person of reasonable firmness present at the scene to fear for his personal safety, each of the persons using or threatening violence is guilty of violent disorder."

It should be noted that the persons present need not have a common purpose (*R. v. Mahroof* (C.A., 1988)) but that all 3 must be using or threatening violence (*R. v. McGuigan & Cameron* (C.A., 1991)); that once again it is unnecessary to produce a frightened bystander; and that unlike riot, it is sufficient to intend to threaten violence.

Affray (s.3)

This is intended to penalise fighting in that "a person is guilty of affray if he uses or threatens violence towards another and his conduct is such as would cause a person of reasonable firmness present at the scene to fear for his personal safety."

Again no frightened bystander need be present. The standard is whether a hypothetical bystander of reasonable firmness would fear for his safety. (See *R. v. Davison* (C.A., 1992).) As with sections 1–2, the offence need not be committed in a public place. However, unlike the other offences under the Act, the violence must be directed against the person and must be more than mere threatening words. (*R. v. Robinson* (D.C., 1993).)

Threatening behaviour (s.4)

This replaced section 5 of the Public Order Act 1936 which had long been the main public order offence and which had been used in a wide range of situations including demonstrations, football hooliganism, "streaking" and industrial disputes.

> "A person is guilty of an offence if he
> (a) uses towards another person, threatening, abusive or insulting words or behaviour, or
> (b) distributes or displays to another person any writing, sign . . . which is threatening, abusive or insulting . . . with intent to cause another to believe that immediate violence will be used . . . or to provoke (such) violence."

The consequences feared or provoked must be immediate, unlawful violence not violence at some unspecified future time. (*R. v. Horseferry Road Stipendiary Magistrate, ex p. Siadatan* (D.C., 1991).)

The phrase "threatening, abusive or insulting" is likely to be interpreted as under the Public Order Act 1936. In *Brutus v. Cozens* (H.L., 1973) Lord Reid said that the words must be given their ordinary English meaning. They must be more than vigorous or unmannerly. The audience must feel threatened, abused or insulted.

Under section 6(3) a person is guilty of an offence under section 4 only if he intends his words, behaviour or writing, etc., to be threatening, abusive or insulting or is aware that it may be threatening, abusive or insulting. (*D.P.P. v. Clarke* (D.C., 1991).) The offence can be committed in public or private, but the act is drafted in such a way as to exclude domestic disputes (s.4(2)). (See *Atkin v. D.P.P.* (D.C., 1989).) It should be noted that in this offence we are not dealing with the hypothetical bystander. The conduct must be directed to another person and it is the reactions of that other person which matter. The speaker must take his audience as he finds it (*Jordan v. Burgoyne* (H.C., 1963)).

Intentionally causing harassment alarm or distress (s.4A)

Section 154 of the 1994 Act creates a new offence which was designed primarily to deal with cases of serious racial harassment although not confined to use in this context. It makes it an offence to intentionally cause harassment alarm or distress by using threatening, abusive or insulting words or behaviour. It is seen as more serious than the s.5 offence and attracts a maximum penalty of six month's imprisonment or a level 5 fine or both.

Offensive conduct (s.5)

This is used for minor acts of disorder such as shouting and swearing which are likely to cause alarm or distress, displaying abusive or insulting slogans or throwing over dustbins and banging on doors in the common parts of blocks of flats. It would cover those minor disturbances formerly dealt with under section 5 of the Public Order Act 1936 but also types of anti-social behaviour which have not been criminalised in the past.

'A person is guilty of an offence if he—

(a) uses threatening, abusive or insulting words or behaviour, or disorderly behaviour, or

(b) displays any writing sign or visible representation which is threatening, abusive or insulting, within the hearing or sight of a person likely to be caused harassment alarm or distress thereby."

In *D.P.P. v. Clarke, Lewis, O'Connell & O'Keefe* (D.C., 1992) it was held that, for a conviction, the accused must intend their behaviour to be threatening etc., or be aware that it might be.

Section 5(4) gives the police the power of summary arrest for this offence, if the person persists in the conduct after being warned to stop. (See *Groom v. D.P.P.* (H.C., 1991).)

The imprecision of this offence has caused concern. It is felt that it leaves the police too great a discretion as to what type of conduct is unacceptable and, indeed, a recent research study has shown wide variation in its use from one police force to another. In the context of a demonstration or industrial dispute, participants may well shout slogans which are abusive and are likely to cause distress to those who disagreed with the cause in question. The Law Commission proposing the offence had confined it to situations where the alarm or distress experienced was "substantial" but this requirement was dropped from the Act itself. The court in *D.P.P. v. Orum* (D.C., 1989), accepted that, in appropriate circumstances police officers could be caused the necessary "harassment, alarm or distress." In fact the greatest single use of the section relates to insults directed at the police.

Other Public Order Offences

Sections 1 and 2 of the 1936 Act make:

(i) the wearing of a uniform signifying association with a political organisation or with the promotion of any political objective, an offence. For the rather wide definition of "uniform" see O'Moran v. D.P.P. (H.C., 1975).

(ii) the organisation or training of a body whose purpose is either

(a) to usurp the function of the police or the armed forces; or

(b) to use or display force in an attempt to achieve a political objective, an offence.

The Public Order Act 1986 does not codify the law and must be seen against a background of common law. There remain a number of other offences which can be used in a public order situation. These include obstructing the police in the execution of their duty (See *Duncan v. Jones* (1936)); obstructing the Highway under s.137 of the Highways Act 1980; note also the use of binding over orders.

RESPONSIBILITY FOR THE POLICE

There is no national police force in Britain. Instead there are local forces historically based on the counties with various amalgamations. In London there is the Metropolitan Police and the City of London Police. Although essentially separate and independent, they share a number of resources including the central criminal record department, the police national computer and the national reporting centre. There is a national pay structure and terms and conditions of employment.

Traditionally responsibility for the police has been shared between the Home Secretary, the local Police Authority and the Chief Officer of Police, that is the Metropolitan Police Commissioner or the Chief Constable. This tripartite structure was established by the Police Act 1964.

The Chief Constable
The Chief Officer of Police has operational control and as will be seen the courts have been extremely unwilling to interfere with the way he settles general policies and concentrates his resources. The 1993 White Paper, "Police Reform: Police Service for the 21st Century", promised that Chief Constables would be given even greater freedom to manage their force in order to provide a service which matched local priorities. It has been argued that the effect of the Police and Magistrates Court Act 1994 has been to restrict their powers. The Act provides for the setting of national and local objectives and performance targets. The Chief Constable has to produce an annual policing plan within these.

Police Authorities
Under the 1964 Act police authorities were committees of the local authority consisting of magistrates and councillors having a responsibility under s.4(1) of the Act to maintain an adequate and efficient police force. This rather vague section was interpreted as giving them particular responsibilities for buildings and equipment. Increasingly some police authorities attempted to use these

powers to influence the style of policing in their area, e.g. by refusing to pay for riot control equipment as they disapproved of the more militaristic style of response to disturbances. (Their ability to do this was severely restricted by the decision in *R. v. Home Secretary, ex p. Northumbria Police Authority* (C.A., 1988)).

The composition of police authorities was controversially altered by the 1994 Act. There will normally be 17 members, 9 councillors, 3 magistrates and 5 independent members appointed by the Authority from a list of suitable candidates. The complex procedure introduced to draw up this list resulted from concern that the independent members would be, in reality, Home Secretary appointees.

Their function is now contained in a new section 4 of the 1964 Act which says that it shall be the duty of the police authority to secure the maintenance of an efficient and effective police force for its area. It must have regard for national objectives set each year by the Home Secretary and its own local objectives, performance targets and its local policing plan the draft of which will have been produced by the Chief Constable. The final plan will contain a statement of the police authority's priorities and financial allocations.

The Government has argued that this gives police authorities an enhanced role. Critics have argued that, in practice, the Home Secretary has increased his power and influence. It has been said that police authorities are left with the problem of trying to balance national and local objectives, that they have been given responsibility without power yet have no real control over the resources available.

The Home Secretary

Under the 1964 Act the Home Secretary performed the following functions:

(a) Some degree of control over the appointment and dismissal of senior officers. (He blocked the appointment of a proposed Chief Constable in Derbyshire in 1990 on the ground that the proposed candidate lacked the necessary experience of other forces.)

(b) He exercises financial controls. (The 1994 Act reduces his control over details of local expenditure.)

(c) He has control over central training.

(d) He has wide powers to make regulations governing all police officers under sections 33 and 37.

(e) He exercises control and influence through his Inspectors of Constabulary who inspect and report on the efficiency of the various forces and who ensure that new knowledge and up to date techniques are brought to the attention of the various forces.

For a number of years it has been argued that the Home Secretary was exercising increased power over the police. It was alleged, for example, that during the Miners' Strike where there was considerable movement of police from one force's area to another with manpower needs and tactics determined centrally, the country had moved towards a national police force under the direct control of central government. Formally, matters were co-ordinated by ACPO (The Association of Chief Police Officers), but to what extent was that body acting under government instructions?

The provisions of the 1994 Act could be used by the Home Secretary to increase his powers still further especially through his power to set national objectives and performance targets. Commentators have argued that it represents a move from guidance to statutory control.

The Courts

Lord Denning in *R. v. Metropolitan Police Commissioner, ex p. Blackburn* (C.A., 1968), stressed that the Chief Officer of Police should be and was independent of the executive. Yet Lord Scarman in his report on the Brixton riots in 1981 argued that while maintaining their independence, the police must be accountable to the community. It has been noted that there is no authority for police authorities undertaking this role. Nor have the courts seemed willing to take on this task. In *R. v. Metropolitan Police Commissioner, ex p. Blackburn* (C.A., 1968), Lord Denning said that while chief officers of police are answerable to law, there are many fields in which they have a discretion with which the law will not interfere. "It is for the Chief Constable ... to decide in any particular case whether enquiries should be pursued or whether an arrest should be made ... It must be for him to decide on the disposition of his force and the concentration of his resources on any particular crime or area. No court can or should give him direction upon such a matter. He can also make policy decisions and give effect to them ..." In *R. v. Chief Constable of Devon and Cornwall, ex p. C.E.G.B.* (C.A., 1981) the court refused to issue a mandamus ordering the Chief Constable to assist the C.E.G.B. in clearing a site of demonstrators who were impeding survey work for a new nuclear power station. The court said that it could not tell the Chief Constable how he should respond to the situation as it could not judge the explosiveness of the situation at the time.

The courts have also refused to interfere with a policy direction not to enforce a particular law. In *R. v. Metropolitan Police Commissioner, ex p. Blackburn No. 3* (C.A., 1973) it was alleged that the Metropolitan Police Commissioner had issued an illegal policy directive in ordering his men not to enforce the provisions of the Obscene Publications Act 1959. The court refused to issue an order of mandamus on the ground that it had not been established that such a blanket directive had been issued and that it was within his rights to deploy his forces as he wished.

Quite clearly, however, he does not have unlimited discretion. He has a duty to enforce the law of the land. So, for example, the courts have indicated that they would interfere if a Chief Constable decided not to take action against housebreakers in any circumstances. (See also *R. v. Oxford, ex p. Levey* (H.C., 1987).)

The Chief Constable's freedom of action has also been limited by E.C. law. In *R. v. Chief Constable of Sussex* (D.C., 1995) the Chief Constable's decision to restrict the protection given to a company transporting veal calves to a limited number of days, was found to be contrary to article 34 of the EC Treaty (which prohibits restrictions on exports between member states). The court accordingly granted an application for judicial review of that decision.

One response to Lord Scarman's recommendations that the police should be more accountable to the community has been the establishment of *police liaison committees*. Many forces introduced these in the early 1980s and these are now mandatory under section 106 of PACE. Police authorities are required to obtain the views of the community on policing in the area. The Act does not specify what arrangements are to be made. (It is more specific about arrangements in the Metropolitan Police District.)

Police Authorities have in fact proceeded in accordance with Home Office guidelines, and committees have been established at sub-divisional level with a membership drawn from representatives of the police authority, justices of the peace, and representatives of the local community. Discussions have related to the incidence of crime in the area and the police response to it. Although there may be discussion of specific types of offence, the committees are not empowered to discuss individual cases or deal with complaints against individual officers. They have no power to take any action and it appears that their potential to increase the level of accountability and to develop policing by consent is minimal.

6. JUDICIAL REVIEW

If an individual has suffered a grievance at the hands of a public body, he may be able to obtain redress through the courts. In addition to any statutory rights of appeal, there may be a right to invoke the inherent supervisory jurisdiction of the High Court. This enables the Court to review the decisions of government ministers, inferior courts, tribunals and other administrative bodies to ensure that they do not act illegally, irrationally or commit some procedural impropriety (*per* Lord Diplock in *C.C.S.U. v. The Minister for the Civil Service* (H.L., 1984)). It must be stressed that the courts are not challenging the merits of the decision but rather whether it is a decision the body is entitled to make, a point emphasised by Lord Scarman in *Nottinghamshire C.C. v. Secretary of State for the Environment* (H.L., 1986), when he said "Judicial review is a great weapon in the hands of the judges; but the judges must observe the constitutional limits set by our parliamentary system on their exercise of this beneficient power."

Historically, the basis of the court's intervention was the *ultra vires* doctrine. If a body exercising statutory powers went beyond the four corners of the Act, then the court could intervene. This might occur in a number of ways. For example, the body might be exercising the wrong powers or may be taking the wrong type of decision. In *Att.-Gen. v. Fulham Corporation* (H.C., 1921) the Local Authority had power under the Baths and Wash Houses Acts 1846–1878 to establish baths, wash houses and open bathing places. The court held that this did not give it the power to operate a commercial laundry. The court must consider what is the area over which power is given. Any exercise of power by the authority which falls outside that area will be *ultra vires*.

Then again a statute might prescribe that the power should be exercised by a named person or a person with specific qualifications. If the power is exercised by another it may be an *ultra vires* act which is a nullity. In *Anisminic v. Foreign Compensation Commission* (C.A., 1968), Lord Diplock described such misuse of power as *excess of jurisdiction*.

The doctrine of *ultra vires* was used not simply to control the scope of the power being exercised but also to control the way it was used. So where a body used its power in a manifestly unreasonable manner, acted in bad faith, refused to take relevant factors into account in reaching its decision or based its decision on irrelevant ones, the court would intervene on the ground that the body had abused its power. (See Lord Reid in *Anisminic* (H.L., 1969).) The basis of the control was that the courts considered that when Parliament gave a body statutory power to act, it could be implied that Parliament intended it to act in a particular way; in good faith, in a reasonable manner, in accordance with the requirements of natural justice. It must be said, however, that in attempting to control such abuse of power, the courts blurred the distinction between the merits of the decision and its *vires*. This could be seen particularly in case such as *Congrieve v. The Home Office* (C.A., 1976).

In recent years the courts have extended their supervisory jurisdiction to include the exercise of prerogative powers. The language of *ultra vires* is therefore no longer appropriate.

THE BASIS OF INTERVENTION

In the *C.C.S.U.* case, Lord Diplock categorised the basis of intervention as follows:

Illegality

"By illegality as a ground for judicial review I mean that the decision maker must understand correctly the law that regulates his decision making power and must give effect to it." (*per* Lord Diplock in *C.C.S.U.*, above).

Thus where power is exercised by someone who does not meet the qualifications laid down in the grant of power, the act may be considered illegal.

In *Allingham v. The Minister of Agriculture and Fisheries* (H.C., 1948) the Minister had a statutory power to give directions regarding the cultivation of land for agricultural purposes. He had an express power to delegate this function to a committee which, in turn, attempted to further sub-delegate its functions to an executive officer who issued a directive to a farmer that only sugar should be grown in a particular field. The farmer failed to comply with the direction and, when fined, challenged its validity alleging that the executive officer had no power to issue it. The court quashed the conviction finding that only the Minister or the Committee had the power to issue such orders under the statute. In *R. v. D.P.P., ex p. Association of First Division Civil Servants* (D.C., 1988) the delegation of certain functions under the Prosecution of Offences Act to non-lawyers was held to be unlawful.

(*N.B.* The courts will sometimes imply a power to sub-delegate into a statutory provision.) In *Vine v. The National Dock Labour Board*

(H.L., 1957) Lord Somervell of Harrow said that in deciding whether there is such a power, two factors have to be considered:

(a) the nature of the power;
(b) the character of the person.

If the power is of a routine nature the courts will be more willing to imply a power to sub-delegate than if there is a strong element of discretion involved. They have also shown themselves reluctant to allow any sub-delegation of judicial or legislative powers. If the body exercising the power has been established especially for that purpose, the courts are likely to conclude that Parliament intended the body to act personally. Where the power is exercised by a minister, for practical reasons, the courts are more willing to hold that he has an implied power to sub-delegate. (*Carltona v. Commissioner of Works* (C.A., 1943).) It should be noted however, that often when a minister acts through his civil servants, there is no delegation. The civil servant is simply acting as the alter ego of the minister. (*R. v. Secretary of State for the Home Office, ex p. Oladehinde* (H.L., 1990).)

Illegality might also consist of using powers in a manner totally different from that envisaged, as in *Att.-Gen. v. Fulham Corporation* (above). Essentially the task of the court is to determine the nature of the powers granted. In *Commissioners of Customs and Excise v. Cure & Deeley* (H.C., 1961), Sachs J. said that in carrying out its task, the court was bound to examine "the nature, the objects and scheme of the parent act, and in the light of that examination, to consider what is the area over which power is given." In doing this, there are a number of presumptions of statutory interpretation which can assist the court such as the presumption that a body has no power to act retrospectively and the presumption that a body has no power to restrict a person's access to the courts. (*Chester v. Bateson* (H.C., 1920).) Cases such as *Bromley L.B.C. v. G.L.C.* (H.L., 1982) demonstrate that determining the scope of a body's power is far from being a mechanical task but involves the court in making value judgments.

There may often be a requirement that before a body exercises its power a particular state of affairs must exist as a preliminary requirement. If power is exercised without this, the action may be illegal. In *White and Collins v. Minister of Health* (C.A., 1939) the Local Authority had certain powers of compulsory purchase in relation to land which did not form part of private parkland. This meant that a condition for the exercise of the power was that the land was of the appropriate type. The court held that an attempt by the Local Authority to acquire private parkland was *ultra vires*. In *Daymond v. South Western Water Authority* (H.L., 1976) water authorities had a power to impose charges on customers, but an attempt to charge persons not connected to mains drainage was held to be *ultra vires* as the correct state of affairs did not exist as a precondition to the exercise of the power.

Irrationality
Irrationality was the second ground on which Lord Diplock would exercise his powers of review.

> "It applies to a decision which is so outrageous in its defiance of logic or of accepted moral standards that no sensible person who had applied his mind to the question to be decided could have arrived at it."

This would appear to cover those situations described in *Anisminic* under the heading of abuse of power although it has been argued that the House of Lords was intending to cut down the opportunities for intervention.

Irrelevant considerations
If a body acting under statutory authority takes an irrelevant consideration into account or ignores a relevant consideration then the resultant decision will be *ultra vires* (*Associated Provincial Picture Houses Ltd. v. Wednesbury Corp.* (C.A., 1948)).

In *Padfield v. Minister of Agriculture and Fisheries* (H.L., 1968) the Minister had the power to refer complaints about the operation of the Milk Marketing Board scheme to a committee. He refused to refer a complaint of substance to the committee. It subsequently emerged that one reason for his decision was that he had taken into account the fact that publicity about the complaint would be politically damaging for the Government at that time. This, the court said, was an irrelevant consideration which rendered his decision unlawful. Lord Upjohn said that unlawful behaviour might be constituted by:

(a) an outright refusal to consider the relevant matter;
(b) a misdirection on a point of law;
(c) taking into account some wholly irrelevant or extraneous consideration;
(d) wholly omitting to take into account a relevant consideration. In *R. v. Somerset C.C., ex p. Fewings* (C.A., 1994) a local authority decision to ban stag hunting on its land was quashed. Under its statutory power it was required to take an objective judgment about the proper management of its land. Clearly the ban was

imposed because hunting was seen as being morally repulsive. This
was an irrelevant consideration.

Essentially the court is concerned whether the decision-making
body has addressed itself to all relevant factors. It is not concerned
with the question whether proper weight has been given to those
factors. (*Pickwell v. Camden London B.C.* (H.C., 1983).) But where
the decision is reached on the basis of two quite separate considerations, one which is relevant and one which the authority is not
entitled to take into account, the court must decide which was the
dominant consideration. If this is an irrelevant consideration then
the authority's action will be reviewable (*R. v. I.L.E.A., ex p.
Westminster Council* (H.C., 1986)).

Improper purpose

The courts have held that if a public body exercises its statutory
power for an improper purpose they can intervene. In *Padfield*'s case
Lord Reid pointed out that Parliament had given the Minister a
discretion as to whether complaints were referred to the committee. It was not, however, an unlimited discretion. He argued that
it could be implied that it had been given with the intention that
it should be used to promote the policy and objects of the enabling
act.

In *R. v. Secretary of State for Foreign Affairs, ex p. World Development
Movement Ltd.* (D.C., 1994), the court held that the Foreign Secretary had used his power to grant overseas aid for an improper purpose. It should have been used to promote development. There was,
however, no economic argument in favour of the proposal. The
reasons were purely political.

One difficulty is how the courts ascertain the policy of any Act
of Parliament. Rarely is this expressed in the statute. Following
the decision in *Pepper v. Hart*, Lord Reid said that the courts must
carry out this task by construing the Act as a whole. Sometimes it
is impossible to determine the purpose and no intervention is possible on this ground as, for example, in *British Oxygen Co. Ltd. v.
Minister of Technology* (H.L., 1971). On the other hand, in *Congrieve
v. The Home Office* (C.A., 1976) the Minister had a statutory power
under the Wireless Telegraphy Act 1949 to revoke television
licences. He used this apparently unrestricted power to revoke
licences purchased early to avoid an increase. The court held that
the Minister had acted *ultra vires* in that he had used his power for
an improper purpose. Lord Denning said that it could be implied
that the Minister had been given this power to enable him to
revoke licences obtained illegally. The licences in question had not

been obtained illegally. The Minister wished to revoke them only to ensure he obtained the expected revenue from the increased cost. The revocations were accordingly of no legal effect.

Bad faith

Although this has clearly been recognised as a ground of challenge for abuse of power, it is difficult to find examples where it stands alone as the ground for attacking the decision. Rather it is an additional line of argument in cases where reliance is being placed on the fact that the decision is unreasonable or that irrelevant considerations have been taken into account. See, *e.g. Webb v. Minister of Housing and Local Government* (C.A., 1965).

Unreasonableness

In *Associated Provincial Picture Houses Ltd. v. Wednesbury Corp.* (C.A., 1948) Lord Greene M.R. stated that decisions could also be challenged on the ground that they were unreasonable. It has been pointed out that "unreasonableness" has been used in two ways in this area:

(a) in an "umbrella" sense where it has been used as a synonym for abuse of power covering the various aspects of abuse of power already mentioned;

(b) in a substantive sense where it means manifest unreasonableness, a decision or exercise of power that is so unreasonable that no reasonable man would agree with it. A widely used example is that of a local authority which ruled that in no circumstances would it employ a teacher with red hair.

Unreasonableness has been used as a ground of challenge in a number of contexts:

(a) To control the exercise of discretion as in the *Wednesbury* case. In practice, the courts do not like to rely on unreasonableness alone but rather to base the decision on the fact that irrelevant considerations have been taken into account, etc. (see *Bromley London B.C. v. GLC* (H.L., 1983)).

(b) To challenge the validity of delegated legislation. Here, in extreme cases, the courts appear willing to rely on this ground of challenge alone. (*Kruse v. Johnson* (H.C., 1898).) The Chief Justice did however stress that a bye-law would not be held to be unreasonable simply because a particular judge thought that it went further than was prudent or necessary or convenient. For an example of a successful challenge see *R. v. H.M. Treasury, ex p. Smedley* (C.A., 1985).

(c) Sometimes reasonableness arises in the context of a precondition before an administrative action can be taken. For example in *Secretary of State for Education and Science v. Tameside Metropolitan B.C.* (H.L., 1977) the Minister had power to take over certain education functions only if satisfied that the local education authority was acting unreasonably. The House of Lords held that the minister could only intervene if there were reasonable grounds, namely that the education authority was acting in a way no other education authority would act. This was also the basis of the court's intervention in *R. v. Secretary of State for the Environment, ex p. Norwich C.C.* (C.A., 1982).

There is, as yet, no recognition of a general duty to give reasons for a decision and it cannot be automatically inferred from their absence that a decision is unreasonable. However the courts are increasingly willing to imply a duty, especially in the case of courts and tribunals (*e.g. R. v. Snaresbrook Crown Court, ex p. Leas* (D.C., 1994). It has also been pointed out that the 1993 Code for Open Government means that the duty will be more readily implied in an administrative context involving Central Government.

Procedural impropriety

Breach of express procedural requirement

The court may review a decision where there has been a failure to comply with express procedural requirements contained in an Act of Parliament or secondary legislation. Examples of such requirements are:

(a)   consultation (*R. v. Social Services Secretary, ex p. Association of Metropolitan Authorities* (H.C., 1986)).
(b)   the holding of an inquiry to hear objections to a planning application (*Jackson Stansfield v. Butterworth* (C.A., 1948)).

The effect of non-compliance with a procedural requirement varies, depending on its importance. Traditionally the courts have categorised requirements as either mandatory or directory. Only where the breach is considered to be of a mandatory procedural requirement will non-compliance affect the validity of the exercise of power as in *Agricultural Training Board v. Aylesbury Mushrooms* (H.C., 1972). Breach of a directory requirement will not affect validity (*R. v. Sheer Metalcraft Ltd.* (H.C., 1948)).

The process of determining whether a particular procedural requirement is mandatory or directory is one of statutory interpretation. What does Parliament intend to be the result of the breach? Of course, Parliament rarely provides express guidance and the court must assess the importance of the requirement and its relationship to the general purpose of the statutory framework in which it is set. (Lord Penzance in *Howard v. Bodington* (H.L., 1877).)

However, in *London & Clydeside Estates Ltd. v. Aberdeen D.C.* (H.L.,

1980), Lord Hailsham criticised a too rigid distinction between mandatory and directory procedural requirements. Not only was it often difficult to ascertain Parliament's intention but the significance of a breach might vary with the circumstances of each case. He said that the court was faced with a spectrum of possibilities. At one end there were serious procedural defects which would render any decision a nullity. Other defects were so trivial as to have no effect. But in the middle, cases would arise where the courts had to exercise their discretion, cases where differences of degree merged almost imperceptibly into differences of kind.

Thus in *Secretary of State for Trade and Industry v. Langridge* (C.A., 1991), Balcombe L.J. considered the following in determining the effect of non-compliance with a procedural requirement:

    (i) the importance of the relevant procedural requirement;
    (ii) the relation of that requirement to the general object intended to be secured by the Act; and
    (iii) the relevant circumstances of the case.

Breach of implied procedural requirement

The court may review a decision for breach of an implied procedural requirement. The most important such requirement is compliance with the rules of natural justice.

Natural justice

The common law has developed two rules of natural justice:

    1. The *Nemo Judex* rule—no man should be a judge in his own cause.
    2. The *Audi Alteram Partem* rule—the right to a fair hearing.

When do the rules of natural justice apply?

Traditionally they were applied to judicial decisions taken by inferior courts and tribunals. In the nineteenth century they were applied to all types of administrative bodies such as public boards and local authorities and to decisions such as licensing, dismissals from office or compulsory purchase. The width of the application of the rules can be seen in *Board of Education v. Rice* (H.L., 1911).

The application of the rules was, however, greatly restricted following the decision in *R. v. Electricity Commissioners, ex p. London Electricity Joint Committee Co. Ltd.* (C.A., 1924) where a *dictum* of Atkin L.J. was interpreted in such a way as to exclude the rules unless:

    (a) the decision being taken affected an individual's legal rights;
    (b) the decision was being taken by a body which had a duty to act judicially.

This encouraged the courts to draw a rigid distinction between judicial and administrative decisions. They imposed a two-fold test that the decision must both affect a person's legal rights and also be taken by a court-like body. So, for example, natural justice was excluded in licensing decisions (*Nakkuda Ali v. Jayaratne* (P.C., 1951)) as a licence was a privilege and not a right, and in the case of a board exercising a disciplinary function (*ex p. Fry* (H.C., 1954)).

The case of *Ridge v. Baldwin* (H.L., 1964) opened up the application of the rules of natural justice to a much wider range of circumstances. The Chief Constable of Brighton was dismissed from office by the Brighton Watch Committee without an adequate hearing. Did natural justice apply? The decision clearly affected the Chief Constable's legal right for no better reason than that it would affect pension rights. It could, however, be argued that the Watch Committee was acting in an executive or administrative capacity rather than judicially.

Lord Reid, in a judgment which presaged a return to a much wider application of the rules, criticised the interpretation placed on Lord Atkin's words in the *Electricity Commissioner's* case. He felt that Lord Atkin had been attempting to explain what was meant by a judicial decision but unfortunately his words had encouraged subsequent courts to concentrate on the form rather than the essence of the decision. The two-fold test was not backed up by the authorities. It was sufficient that the decision affected a person's rights.

The importance of the decision lies in the fact that it indicated that natural justice applied to all decisions affecting a person's rights irrespective of the form of the decision-making process or the nature of the body entrusted with the decision. It was left to subsequent decisions to extend the application of the rules still further to those decisions which did not affect a person's legal rights but regulated the grant of a privilege, etc.

This was done in the following ways:

(a) By extending the concept of legal right. In *Nagle v. Fielden* (C.A., 1966) Lord Denning applied the rules of natural justice to a refusal of a licensing application on the ground that the applicant had, by virtue of the refusal, been deprived of her right to work. See also Denning M.R. in *R. v. Barnsley M.B.C., ex p. Hook* (C.A., 1976).

(b) By applying natural justice in situations where there was "a right, an interest, a legitimate expectation of being granted a hearing"—*per* Denning M.R. in *Schmidt v. Secretary of State for Home Affairs* (C.A., 1969). So, for example, in disciplinary hearings, natural justice has been held to apply on the ground that, as allegations have been made against a person, justice demands a right to answer these allegations. (*R. v. Hull Prison, Board of Visitors, ex p. St. Germain* (C.A., 1979).) The courts have also been willing to apply the rules to various licensing decisions on the ground that the applicant had a legitimate expectation of being granted a hearing. (*R. v. Gaming Board, ex p. Benaim and Khaida* (C.A., 1970).) See also *C.C.S.U. v. Minister for the Civil Service* (H.L., 1985).

In *McInnes v. Onslow Fane* (H.C., 1978) a contrast was drawn between cases involving forfeiture of a licence (natural justice applied as there was a right to answer any allegations which had been brought), renewal cases (where in view of the fact that a person's livelihood would be affected if the renewal was not granted, there is a legitimate expectation of being given a hearing), and initial applications where minimal standards of fairness apply.

Where a person is deprived of some status as a result of allegations, the courts have applied the rules on the basis that there is a legitimate expectation of a hearing. (*Stevenson v. United Road Transport Union* (C.A., 1976).)

(c) The courts will readily imply the rules of natural justice into a statutory framework. See, *e.g. Malloch v. Aberdeen Corp.* (H.L., 1971).

In what circumstances has natural justice been excluded?

Policy grounds. A restricted right to a hearing was upheld by the Court of Appeal in *R. v. Secretary of State for the Home Department, ex p. Hosenball* (1977). It concerned a challenge to a deportation order. Lord Denning restricted the full application of the rules of natural justice on the ground of national security.

The restriction on the application of the rules to disciplinary hearings involving prisoners was removed by the *St. Germain* case, where the hearing was conducted by the Board of Visitors. Even disciplinary decisions taken by the prison governor could be reviewable (see *Leech v. Deputy Governor of Parkhurst* (H.L., 1988)).

As can be seen below, in administrative decision making, where the application of the rules of natural justice might be inappropriate, there may be an implied requirement to follow a fair procedure which might lead to the same result.

1. The Nemo Judex Rule—the rule against bias.

If the judge has a pecuniary interest in the outcome of a case then he is absolutely barred from hearing it. There is no need to show bias. The mere existence of the interest is sufficient to disqualify the judge—*Dimes v. Grand Junction Canal* (H.L., 1852). The interest must not be too remote. *R. v. Rand* (H.C., 1866).

Other non-pecuniary interests may disqualify a judge from acting, for example:

(a) family relationships—*Metropolitan Properties v. Lannon* (C.A., 1969);
(b) business connection—*R. v. Sussex Justices, ex p. McCarthy* (H.C., 1924);
(c) judge also acting as prosecutor—*ex p. Hook*.

The test of bias. Where there is a non-pecuniary interest it is not necessary to establish actual bias but it is necessary to show that the decision has given the appearance of bias. In *Sussex Justices* the court said that "it is of fundamental importance that justice should not only be done but should manifestly and undoubtedly be seen to be done."

How is the test formulated? In *R. v. Gough* (H.L., 1994) the House resolved a conflict between the authorities and established the following test: Was there a real danger of bias by the decision-maker. This was further explained in *R. v. Inner West London Coroner, ex p. Dallaglio* (C.A., 1994) where the court said: "In reaching its conclusion the court personified the reasonable man."

The question to be determined was whether there was a real danger, meaning a real risk or real possibility of injustice having occurred as a result of bias.

2. The audi alteram partem rule—the right to a fair hearing

It is impossible to lay down precisely the contents of this rule as this may vary depending on the circumstances and the type of function being exercised.

The minimum requirement is that the person must have an adequate opportunity of presenting his case. (*Local Government Board v. Arlidge* (H.L., 1915).) This does not mean that a person is always entitled to an oral hearing. (*R. v. Housing Appeal Tribunal* (H.C., 1920).)

The courts are concerned to see that there is equality of treatment between the parties. So, for example, the rule was broken when the court heard one side in the absence of the other. (*Errington v. Minister of Health* (C.A., 1935).) A person must also have adequate notice of any charges to be brought against him or any matters that have to be taken into account. (*Kanda v. Government of Malaya* (P.C., 1962).) The court said:

"If the right to be heard is a real right which is worth anything, it must carry with it a right in the accused man to know the case which is made against him. He must know what evidence has been given and what statements have been made affecting him, and then he must be given a fair opportunity to correct or contradict them."

In *R. v. Secretary of State for the Home Department, ex p. Georghiades* (D.C., 1992), the court said that justice and fairness required that a prisoner should be told why his parole licence had been revoked to enable him to present his case to the Parole Board.

A person must have a reasonable time to prepare his case. In *R. v. Thames Magistrates, ex p. Polemis* (H.C., 1974) the court held that if a person had been given insufficient time, an adjournment must be granted.

The tribunal need not always observe the strict procedures of a court of justice. In *R. v. Commissioner for Racial Equality, ex p. Cottrell* (H.C., 1980) it was said that as the function being exercised was more administrative than judicial the attendance and cross-examination of witnesses, from whom statements had been taken, at a formal hearing was unnecessary. Contrast this with *R. v. Board of Visitors of Hull Prison, ex p. St. Germain No. 2* (H.C., 1979) where it was said that persons charged with serious disciplinary offences had a right to call any evidence which was likely to assist in establishing vital facts in issue, that the chairman had a discretion to refuse to call witnesses to prevent the accused calling so many witnesses as to make the system unworkable but that fairness demanded that there be a right to cross-examine witnesses.

The courts do not appear to consider that legal representation is an absolute requirement of the rule although there is a readiness to imply it if procedural rules are silent. Lord Denning has gone further than any other judge in demonstrating a willingness to require legal representation even where this is prohibited by the procedural rules governing the body in question. (See, *e.g. Pett v. Greyhound Racing Association* (C.A., 1969).) His views were criticised by the House of Lords, for example in *Pett No. 2* (H.L., 1970) and even he held in *Maynard v. Osmond* (C.A., 1977) that legal representation was not an absolute requirement where a police officer who was facing disciplinary charges was denied legal representation under the Police Disciplinary Regulations. *R. v. Board of Visitors of Wormwood Scrubs Prison, ex p. Anderson* (H.C., 1983) held that the

Board of Visitors should have exercised its discretion to allow legal representation in view of the seriousness of the charges and the potential penalty, the need for fairness between the parties involved and the ability of the prisoners to represent themselves. Other relevant factors might be the complexity of the case and whether any points of law were likely to arise. See also *R. v. Board of Visitors of H.M. Prison, The Maze, ex p. Hone* (H.L., 1988).

3. Implied requirements of fairness

Lord Scarman in the *C.C.S.U.* case spoke of a duty to act fairly even where purely administrative acts were involved. So, for example, there might have been a duty to consult the Union even though this was not expressly prescribed.

In *Wheeler v. Leicester City Council* (H.L., 1985) following the decision of four members of Leicester Rugby Club to tour South Africa, the Local Authority, landlords of the club's ground, banned the club from using the ground for a year because they were dissatisfied with the club's response to its members' actions. This decision was quashed by the House of Lords. Lord Roskill said that the court should interfere because of the unfair manner in which the council set about obtaining its objective and as such fell within Lord Diplock's ground of procedural impropriety. Such "unfairness" may also be considered as "manifest unreasonableness" in the *Wednesbury* sense. (See Lord Templeman in *Wheeler*.)

In *Doody v. Secretary of State for the Home Department* (H.L., 1993) Lord Mustill said that where an Act of Parliament conferred an administrative power there was a presumption that it would be exercised in a manner which was fair in all the circumstances.

Comment

The headings of illegality, irrationality and procedural impropriety provide a convenient means of categorising the circumstances in which the court may exercise its supervisory jurisdiction but the categories are not intended to be exhaustive. In the *C.C.S.U.* case, Lord Diplock foresaw further development on a case by case basis. He suggested in particular that the principle of "proportionality" which is recognised in community law might be incorporated into our law. Proportionality is concerned with balance and whether the means justify the ends. It has been described by the Committee of Ministers of the Council of Europe in 1980 as follows:

"An appropriate balance must be maintained between the adverse effects which an administrative authority's decision may have on the rights, liberties or interests of the person concerned and the purpose which the authority is seeking to pursue."

In *R. v. Secretary of State for the Home Department, ex p. Brind* (H.L., 1991), proportionality was rejected as a discrete ground of challenge although some of their Lordships appeared to recognise proportionality as a factor in determining whether there had been abuse of power.

7. REMEDIES

JUDICIAL REVIEW—THE AVAILABLE REMEDIES

These fall into two groups, the prerogative orders (certiorari, prohibition and mandamus) and the non-prerogative remedies (declaration and injunction).

The prerogative orders
These orders (formerly writs) were originally brought by the King against his officers to compel them to exercise their functions properly or to prevent them abusing their powers. They are remedies of public law and will not lie to control the activities of private bodies or domestic tribunals. Nor will they lie to control the activities of the High Court itself (*R. v. Visitors to the Inns of Court, ex p. Calder* (D.C., 1992)).

Certiorari
Certiorari is used to quash the decisions of inferior courts, tribunals, local authorities and other public bodies, government ministers, etc.;

(a)   on grounds of illegality, irrationality and procedural impropriety;
(b)   where there is error of law on the face of the record.

In *R. v. Northumberland Compensation Appeal Tribunal, ex p. Shaw* (C.A., 1952) the tribunal, assessing the amount of compensation owed to Shaw, misinterpreted the statutory provisions and made an error of law which was apparent on the face of the record of the decision. That decision was quashed.

While formerly confined to judicial decisions affecting a person's legal rights, it has been granted to control licensing decisions (*R. v. Barnsley M.B.C., ex p. Hook* (C.A., 1976); in *R. v. Paddington Valuation Officer, ex p. Peachey Property Corp. Ltd.* (C.A., 1966) to challenge an exercise of power by a valuation officer in compiling the valuation list; and in *R. v. London Borough of Hillingdon, ex p. Royco Homes Ltd.* (H.C., 1974), to quash the granting of planning permission. It would therefore be inaccurate today to say that certiorari would not lie to control the exercise of an administrative function.

Prohibition

Prohibition is used to restrain a tribunal, minister or other public body from proceeding in excess of jurisdiction. For example in *R. v. Liverpool Corp., ex p. Liverpool Taxifleet Operators Association* (C.A., 1972) it was alleged that a local authority had failed to exercise its discretion properly and was about to act illegally in the allocation of taxi cab licences. An order of prohibition was granted to prevent the authority acting on this invalid decision.

In general its scope is similar to that of certiorari although it cannot be used to prevent a tribunal from making an error of law on the face of the record.

Mandamus

Mandamus is an order which commands a person or body to perform a public duty. Typically it is used to compel the exercise of a duty imposed by statute on a public body. For example in *R. v. Manchester Corp.* (H.C., 1911) the order compelled the local authority to make bye-laws that it was under a statutory duty to make.

It would seem that mandamus cannot be directed to the Crown as the Crown is not commandable (*R. v. Secretary of State for War* (C.A., 1891). Nor can it be issued against any servant of the Crown acting in his capacity as servant. But where, by statute, an officer of the Crown has a duty towards a member of the public, mandamus may lie to compel performance of that duty. Thus a distinction is drawn between a duty imposed on the Crown and a duty imposed on a named Crown servant.

Non-prerogative orders

There are two remedies, the declaration and the injunction, which are not primarily remedies of public law but are widely used in this field.

Declaration

A declaration is a convenient and flexible remedy available in both public and private law matters which can be used to obtain a statement of the legal relationship between parties in a wide range of circumstances. It can be used, for example,

(a) to challenge the legality of administrative decisions. (*Ridge v. Baldwin* (H.L., 1964));

(b) to challenge the validity of delegated legislation. (*Daymond v. South West Water Authority* (H.L., 1976));

(c) to establish the existence or the scope of a public duty. (*Central Electricity Board v. Jennaway* (H.C., 1959)).

(d) Declaratory judgments can be made against the Crown.

It is not necessary for the party applying for relief to show that he has some subsisting cause of action or a right to some other relief. (*Gouriet v. Union of Post Office Workers* (H.L., 1978).) *R. v. Secretary of State for Employment, ex p. Equal Opportunities Commission* (H.L., 1994) made it clear that the court still has the power to make a declaratory judgment in judicial review proceedings whether or not it could also make a prerogative order.

Restrictions on the use of the declaration

(a) The applicant must have a right or interest which is justiciable.

(b) There must be a real dispute between the parties. The court will not attempt to resolve an academic matter (*R. v. Secretary of State for Employment, ex p. Equal Opportunities Commission*).

(c) As a declaration will not quash a decision, it cannot be used to challenge a decision on the ground that there has been an error of law on the face of the record of the tribunal's decision as this is an error within jurisdiction. A declaration that such a decision is irregular would still leave the decision intact. *Punton v. Minister of Pensions and National Insurance No. 2* (H.L., 1963).

(d) Interim declarations cannot be made.

Injunction

This is an order by the courts, either prohibiting the party to whom it is addressed from doing a particular act, or requiring the party in question to perform a particular act. Accordingly injunctions can be either prohibitory or mandatory. It can be used:

(a) To prohibit a body from acting *ultra vires*. In *Bradbury v. Enfield L.B.C.* (C.A., 1967) an injunction was granted to prevent a local authority from reorganising local schools without following the correct procedure;

(b) In *Att.-Gen., ex relator McWhirter v. I.B.A.* (C.A., 1973), an application was made for an injunction to restrain breaches of statutory duty;

(c) Mandatory injunctions are much less common in public law as mandamus is normally a more appropriate remedy, but they have been granted, for example, to require public bodies to enforce planning regulations and fire precautions.

Restrictions on the use of the injunction

Under the Crown Proceedings Act 1947, s.21(1), a final injunction will not be awarded against the Crown or one of its officers, although this has little practical importance as the Crown will abide by the terms of a declaration. (The major difficulty has been the inability to obtain interim relief.)

In the express context of Community law, the House of Lords in *Factortame Ltd. (No. 2)* (H.L., 1991), disregarded the rule precluding such interim relief in national law, in order to give protection to the rights claimed under Community law. In *M. v. Home Office* (H.L., 1994), the possibility of interim relief against ministers and government departments acting in the name of the Crown was recognised. The Law Commission Report on Remedies in Administrative Law calls for a clear recognition of this right.

Reform

The recent Law Commission report recommends changes in nomenclature in order to make the function and nature of prerogative orders clear to non-lawyers. It suggests that the terms certiorari, prohibition and mandamus be replaced by quashing, prohibitory and mandatory orders.

APPLICATIONS FOR REVIEW

Up till 1977, the procedures for applying for prerogative and non-prerogative remedies were entirely separate. The remedies themselves were issued from different courts. This meant that litigants had to choose at the outset which route to follow. If the wrong choice was made the action had to start again. This was time consuming and expensive and even, in some cases, led to the action being time barred.

It was difficult to advise at the outset, as to which route should be followed as prerogative and non-prerogative remedies each had their advantages and disadvantages. For example, the rules as to standing were more generous for the prerogative remedies but there were serious procedural disadvantages such as lack of a proper interlocutory process. As a remedy of public law a prerogative order might be refused if the court felt that the dispute was not properly a public law matter, yet there was considerable uncertainty as to the definition of "public law". Prerogative and non-prerogative remedies could not be combined. Thus if the applicant wished to claim damages he had to bring a separate action.

Significant changes were made in 1977 with the introduction of the application for judicial review.

Following this report a number of changes were made to Order 53 of the Rules of the Supreme Court under which applications for prerogative orders are made. This was initially by regulation (S.I. 1977 No. 1955 as amended by 1980 No. 2000) and is now by section 31 of the Supreme Court Act 1981.

The procedure for applying for judicial review

Applicants make an umbrella application for judicial review (AFR). Under this method it is possible to ask for any of the prerogative remedies together with declaration and injunction either singly, in any combination and in the alternative. See, for example, *R. v. The Inland Revenue Commissioners, ex p. Rossminster* (H.L., 1980).

Damages can also be awarded where appropriate. (N.B. No new rights of action were introduced, *Calveley v. Chief Constable of Merseyside Police* (C.A., 1988).)

Applicants do not, therefore, have to choose which route to pursue, and may leave it to the court to provide the most appropriate remedy.

There is a two stage procedure for making the application:

(a) The filter stage.

The applicant makes an *ex parte* application for leave to apply to the Divisional Court under section 31 of the Supreme Court Act 1981 and Order 53 of the Rules of the Supreme Court. The application may be considered at a hearing before a single judge of the Queen's Bench Division or may be considered in private by the judge on the basis of the documents alone. A hearing is likely to be requested if the application involves a point of law likely to require some argument, if interim relief is sought, or if the judge wishes to give guidance on a matter concerning the public interest. The notice of the application will be accompanied by an affidavit containing all the basic factual material on which the application is based.

The purpose of this filter stage is to weed out hopeless cases at the earliest possible time, thus saving pressure on the courts and needless expense for the applicant. In order to obtain leave, the applicant must satisfy the court that he has, on the face of it, an arguable case and has the necessary standing to make the application. Where leave is refused there is provision for renewal of the application and a right of appeal. The exact procedure varies depending on whether it is a civil or criminal matter and whether there has been an oral hearing.

The requirement to seek leave is a significant filter but operates with considerable variation. Some judges examine the application at length at this stage. Others content themselves with a quick look. Research has indicated that no common criteria are being applied. The Law Commission has recommended that the leave stage should revert to being an informal stage, conducted almost entirely on paper. The judge should be able to request further information before deciding whether to allow the application to proceed. There should be clear criteria for the judge to follow.

(b) The hearing.

Once leave has been granted, the applicant must institute a substantive application for judicial review. In a criminal case this will be before the Divisional Court of the Queen's Bench Division and will normally be before two judges. In civil matters the case will normally be heard by a single judge sitting in open court. In very important cases, three judges may sit. The judges will be administrative law specialists from the Crown Office list.

The main source of evidence will be sworn affidavits although the court has the power to take oral evidence and to permit cross-examination. Despite the fact that cross-examination is now expressly allowed, the court's long standing reluctance to permit it appears to have persisted.

Discretionary nature of remedies

The court has a discretion as to whether to grant relief. Factors which might persuade the court to refuse the application are:

(i) the availability of an alternative remedy. (*R. v. Birmingham City Council, ex p. Ferrero Ltd.* (C.A., 1993).) But the alternative remedy may be inappropriate in the circumstances. (*R. v. Chief Constable of Merseyside, ex p. Calveley* (C.A., 1986).)

(ii) where review would serve no useful purpose as the decision, properly taken, would be the same. (*R. v. Monopolies and Mergers Commission, ex p. Argyll Group plc* (C.A., 1986).)

(iii) where the court does not like the motives of the applicant (*R. v. Customs and Excise Commissioners, ex p. Cooke & Stevenson* (H.L., 1970).

(iv) The court may also refuse to intervene on the ground that the matter is non-justiciable. It may decide that judicial procedures are unsuitable to control the administrative action in question e.g. because of considerations of national security. (*Council of Civil Service Unions v. Minister of Civil Service* (H.L., 1985).)

Time limits for making an application

Section 31(6) of the Supreme Court Act 1981 says that the court may refuse a AFR on ground of undue delay if it considers that the granting of the relief would be likely to cause substantial hardship to, or substantially prejudice the rights of, any person, or would be detrimental to good administration. Section 31(6) then has to be read together with Rule 4 of Order 53 which states that an application for certiorari must be brought promptly and in any event within three months from the date when the grounds for the application first arose, unless there is good reason for extending the period within which the application is made. It would therefore appear that:

(a) There is no three month entitlement for certiorari and an application made within the three month period could be refused for delay, for example, if that delay had substantially prejudiced the rights of any person (*R. v. Independent Television Commission, ex p. T.V. NI Ltd.* (C.A., 1991).)

(b) Where an application for certiorari is made after three months the onus is on the applicant to show why the period should be extended. In *R. v. Stratford-on-Avon D.C., ex p. Jackson* (C.A., 1985) the delay in making the application arose mainly because of difficulty in obtaining legal aid. The court was satisfied that the circumstances constituted a good reason for extending the period under Rule 4.

(c) Even if an applicant satisfactorily discharges the burden of showing that there is good reason for extending the three month period, the application may still fail if, under section 31(6) the granting of the relief was, for example, detrimental to good administration (*R. v. Dairy Produce Quota Tribunal, ex p. Caswell* (C.A., 1989)).

The 1994 Law Commission Report, while approving the end result in *Caswell*, notes that the rules are confusing and difficult and should be replaced by a new provision.

The requirements of standing

Only an applicant who has the requisite standing may apply for judicial review. Prior to the 1977 reforms, the test of standing was clearly different for the various remedies. For example, the requirements for obtaining a declaration or an injunction were much stricter than in the case of the prerogative orders as, being also remedies of private law it was normally necessary to show that the applicant's legal rights had been affected in some way. In the case of the prerogative orders there was a wide divergence of opinion as to the requisite test, ranging from that of the "public spirited citizen" (Lord Denning) to the "applicant with some special interest over and above that of the community as a whole" (Lord Parker).

The Law Commission recommended that there should be one test of standing for all the remedies, that an applicant should have such interest as the court considers sufficient in the matter to

which the application relates. Section 31(3) of the Supreme Court
Act 1981 provides that the court will not grant leave for an AFR
unless the applicant has sufficient interest in the matter to which
the application relates.

What constitutes sufficient interest?

The House of Lords considered this in *R. v. I.R.C., ex p. The
National Federation of Self Employed and Small Businesses Ltd.* (1982).
The applicants wished to challenge an alleged amnesty granted to
casual workers in the newspaper industry who had been avoiding
paying tax for many years. Quite clearly this decision did not affect
the applicants' legal rights. But did they have a sufficient interest?

The House of Lords (Lord Diplock dissenting) advised that they
had not. The following points arose.

(a) The majority felt that the applicants' standing could not be
considered in the abstract but only in conjunction with the merits
of the case. Only in a few extreme cases could applications be
weeded out for lack of standing at the filter stage.

(b) Thus a connection was drawn between the sufficiency of the
interest and the seriousness of the illegality complained of. The
more serious the illegality, the more liberal the rules of standing.

(c) Their Lordships were divided as to the extent to which they
were constrained by the pre-1977 authorities in determining the
question of standing. Lord Diplock alone felt that they had an
unfettered discretion. The majority felt that they had to pay some
attention to the earlier law but were divided as to the precise
weight to be accorded to it.

(d) A similar divergence of views was seen on whether there is
a uniform test of standing. Those judges who felt most bound by
the earlier authorities were led to the conclusion that the test
varied from remedy to remedy. In contrast Lords Diplock and Roskill saw the main purpose of the reforms as being to sweep away
procedural differences between the various remedies.

The House of Lords accepted that it was not necessary that the
applicants' legal rights were affected. According to Lord Scarman
the test was whether "there is a genuine grievance reasonably
asserted." He stressed the relationship between the sufficiency of
the applicants' interest in relation to the subject matter of the
application. Lord Fraser emphasised that a mere busybody would
lack sufficient interest but gave little guidance as to how one distin-
guishes the busybody from the person with a reasonable concern.

Decisions since the *I.R.C.* case have confirmed that questions of
standing can rarely be disposed of as preliminary issues. (See *R. v.*

Felixstowe JJ., ex p. Leigh & Another (C.A., 1987).) They have also tended to confirm the view that the House of Lords' interpretation of the test of sufficient interest has liberalised the rules of standing. For example the interest of a business competitor was recognised in *R. v. Department of Transport, ex p. Presvac Engineering Ltd.* (C.A., 1991). So too persons may have the requisite interest as a result of "legitimate expectation that they will be heard," perhaps arising out of assurances given or knowledge of general practice (*O'Reilly v. Mackman* (H.L., 1983)).

In a number of cases the courts have allowed pressure groups to apply for judicial review. Community Associations were successful in convincing the court of their standing in *R. v. Hammersmith & Fulham Borough Council, ex p. People Before Profit Ltd.* (D.C., 1981). In *R. v. Secretary of the Environment, ex p. Rose Theatre Trust Co.* (H.C., 1989) however, archeologists, actors, local residents, the local M.P., and a Trust formed by those persons, did not have sufficient interest to challenge the Secretary of State's refusal to schedule the site of the Rose Theatre as a monument of national importance. In *R. v. Poole Borough Council, ex p. Beebee* (H.L., 1991), individuals representing the Worldwide Fund for Nature had standing. The judge emphasised their long association with the site which was the subject of a planning dispute, and their involvement in the planning application. Similarly in *R. v. H.M. Inspectorate of Pollution, ex p. Greenpeace* (D.C., 1994) it was held that Greenpeace had standing to challenge the variation of existing authorisations for the Sellafield nuclear processing site by reason of its membership in the area.

The Law Commission has recommended that it should be made clear that, in appropriate cases, applications may be brought by interest groups.

Thus in determining whether the applicant has standing the courts consider:

(a) the merits of the application;
(b) the nature of the applicant's interest;
(c) all the circumstances of the case.

Who is amenable to judicial review?

The supervisory jurisdiction of the High Court is over bodies exercising public law functions. Traditionally these bodies have been established by statute or through an exercise of the royal prerogative. In *R. v. City Panel on Take-Overs and Mergers, ex p. Datafin plc* (C.A., 1987), judicial review was sought to challenge the decision of an unincorporated association which exercised no statutory or prerogative powers. Indeed Lord Donaldson MR described it as "a body performing its functions without any means of judicial support."

Despite the Datafin decision, the courts have refused to extend judicial review to control the activities of sporting regulatory bodies such as the Jockey Club or Football Association. They have not however ruled it out completely.

Not every public body will be subject to review with regard to every action it takes. (See *R. v. BBC, ex p. Lavelle* (C.A., 1983) but only if it is a public law matter.)

In *R. v. Chief Rabbi, ex p. Wachmann* (D.C., 1992), the court held that the exercise of a disciplinary function by the chief rabbi was not susceptible to judicial review.

An exclusive procedure?

Clearly the AFR procedure must be used to obtain a prerogative order. But in the case of a declaration or an injunction, does the applicant have the choice in a public law matter whether to proceed by way of action or use the AFR procedure?

In *O'Reilly v. Mackman* (H.L., 1982) an attempt to obtain a declaration by way of action that a Board of Visitors had acted contrary to the rules of natural justice in hearing disciplinary charges against a prisoner, was struck out as an abuse of process. Section 31(2) of the Supreme Court Act 1981 provides that a declaration may be obtained by means of an application for review where the High Court considers it would be just and convenient having regard to:

(a) the nature of the matters in respect of which relief may be granted by way of the prerogative orders;
(b) the nature of the persons and bodies against whom relief may be granted;
(c) all the circumstances of the case.

The court was satisfied that, in the circumstances, relief could have been granted by way of a prerogative order. It was clearly a public law matter. It was felt that in this case it would be more appropriate to use the AFR procedure as it provided certain safe-guards against frivolous applications, for example the need to apply for leave. Their Lordships felt that although the AFR procedure was not the exclusive procedure for raising such a matter it would generally be the most appropriate. As had been pointed out in the Court of Appeal, there was a clear need to develop a comprehensive method of handling such cases and the Divisional Court had particular expertise in the area.

It was suggested that there were three circumstances where the AFR procedure might be inappropriate:

(a) Where the matter was collateral to another application. (Applied in *Cocks v. Thanet D.C.* (H.L., 1982));
(b) Where public law issues are raised as a defence to criminal charges. (See *Wandsworth LBC v. Winder* (C.A., 1985).)
(c) Otherwise on a case-to-case basis. It may be inappropriate to use the AFR procedure in a complex Chancery matter for example.

Subsequent cases led to concern that the existence of a public law element, however slight, should force the citizen to use the AFR procedure and deprive him of the right to bring an action for private law relief. *Roy v. Kensington & Chelsea & Westminster Family Practitioner Committee* (H.L., 1992) represented a retreat from this exclusivity principle. The House of Lords identified two approaches

(i) a broad approach under which Order 53 would only be insisted on if private rights were not in issue.
(ii) a narrow approach which required applicants to proceed by the AFR procedure in all proceedings in which public law matters are challenged subject to those exceptions already noted.

It followed the broad approach and found the fact that there was an incidental public law matter did not prevent the litigant from seeking to establish his right by action. This approach has been approved by the Law Commission in its recent report on Remedies and confirmed by the House of Lords in *R. v. Secretary of State for Employment, ex p. EOC* (H.L., 1994).

Indeed considerable difficulties have been caused by the lack of any comprehensive definition of public law. The mere fact that one of the parties involved is a public body is not, of itself, sufficient. In *R. v. Panel of Take-overs and Mergers, ex p. Datafin plc* (C.A., 1987), the court said that in considering whether it was a public law matter, the court must not only consider the source of a body's powers and duties but also their nature. Do these have a "Public element" or was its sole source of power a "consensual submission to its jurisdiction?"

THE PARLIAMENTARY COMMISSIONER

Following considerable pressure to establish a mechanism to invest-igate complaints by members of the public who felt that they had suffered injustice at the hands of central government, The Parliamentary Commissioner Act 1967 was passed providing for the appointment of a Commissioner to investigate complaints of maladministration by those government bodies and public authorities listed in the Act. The 1967 Act was amended by the Parliamentary and Health Service Commissioners Act 1987. The Parliamentary Commissioner (P.C.) has specific responsibility for Northern Ireland (1969), and for the Health Service (1973). A separate Local Government Commission was established under the Local Government Act 1974 to investigate maladministration by local government departments.

The office

He is a Crown appointment. He holds office during good behaviour, but may be removed by the Crown following addresses from both Houses of Parliament. His status is similar to that of a judge in terms of independence. He has the power to appoint his own staff, subject to Treasury control over numbers and conditions of service.

Terms of reference

To investigate all complaints of maladministration by those departments listed in Schedule 2 of the Act.

The Schedule lists not only the various departments of state such as the Treasury and the Home Office but also government departments such as the Inland Revenue, Customs and Excise Department, and certain non-departmental bodies such as the Arts Council (Parliamentary & Health Service Commissioners Act 1987). The Deregulation and Contracting Out Act 1994 extends his jurisdiction to many agencies which have taken over responsibility for work traditionally done by government departments e.g. the Benefits Agency.

Maladministration

Maladministration is not defined in the Act. It appears that the intention was to allow the P.C. guided by the Select Committee on the Parliamentary Commissioner to work out a practical definition.

In his 1973 Annual Report, the P.C. defined maladministration as "any kind of administrative shortcoming."

Richard Crossman, speaking for the Government during the Second Reading debate on the passage of the Bill through the Commons said, in what has become known as the "Crossman Catalogue" that maladministration might include "bias, neglect, inattention, delay, incompetence, ineptitude, perversity, turpitude, arbitrariness and so on." In *R. v. Local Commissioner for Administration North East England, ex p. Bradford M.C.C.* (C.A., 1979), a case involving the jurisdiction of the Local Commission which has similar terms of reference, Lord Denning accepted the Crossman catalogue as an adequate description of the scope of the term.

At first the P.C. interpreted his terms of reference rather narrowly refusing to question the quality of discretionary decisions even where these appeared biased or perverse. Providing the proper administrative procedures had been followed he would not investigate, however bad the rules appeared. Gradually he has begun to consider such cases, encouraged by the Select Committee. So, for example, if he feels the rule causes hardship or injustice, he will ask the department what action has been taken to review the rule. Failure to carry out such a review adequately might constitute maladministration.

The following have been found to constitute maladministration:

(a) failure to provide necessary information and advice;
(b) failure to provide an adequate explanation;
(c) provision of inadequate or misleading information and advice;
(d) basing decision on false or inadequate information, ignoring relevant evidence;
(e) delay;
(f) failure to follow departmental rules and procedures;
(g) rudeness and inconsiderate behaviour by officials;
(h) bias;
(i) failure to monitor faulty procedures.

Section 12(3) of the Act expressly excludes consideration of the merits of the decision. The rationale for this is that policy matters are the exclusive concern of Parliament. Note, however, the difficulty of distinguishing questions of merit and policy from the way in which the decision has been reached. (*Ex p. Bradford M.C.C.*, above.)

Exclusions

1. The P.C. is excluded from considering those matters listed in the Third Schedule.

These include:

(a) Actions affecting relations with other governments or international organisations.
(b) Actions taken under the Extradition Act 1870 or the Fugitive Offenders Act 1881.
(c) Administration of territories overseas.
(d) Security and passport matters, criminal investigations.
(e) Commencement or conduct of legal proceedings.
(f) The exercise of the prerogative of mercy.
(g) Actions taken in relation to contractual or other commercial transactions excluding certain matters relating to compulsory purchase.
(h) Action taken in respect of appointment, removal, pay, discipline and other personnel matters by those bodies covered by the Act.

(i) The grant of honours, awards and privileges within the gift of the Crown.

Restrictions (g) and (h) have been widely criticised.

2. The P.C. will not normally investigate a matter for which the complainant has a legal remedy before the courts unless there is doubt about its availability or to pursue the remedy would be slow or expensive.

3. The P.C. can only investigate the exercise of administrative functions. He cannot investigate judicial or legislative (section 12(3)).

4. He has refused to investigate matters which he considers to be purely political, *e.g.* the allocation of time between political parties for party political broadcasts.

Investigation of complaints

Complaints must be channelled through M.P.s. As there is concern that this might deter complainants it has been suggested that it should be possible to approach the P.C. directly. The Select Committee rejected this arguing that the P.C. would be overwhelmed with complaints and that it would undermine the role of the M.P. in looking after the interests of his constituents. The response to this might be that if there was a dramatic increase in the number of complaints resources should be made available to deal with them. Not all M.P.s deal with complaints effectively. Indeed they lack the resources to do so. It is surely more important to safeguard the interests of constituents than to pander to the sensibilities of M.P.s. In any event it would not prevent constituents enlisting the help of their M.P. if they so wished.

In fact, since 1978, the P.C. has, if approached directly, offered to send the complaint to an M.P. asking for it to be returned. This appears to work quite satisfactorily.

It should be noted that a complainant can approach any M.P.

A very high proportion of complaints are not investigated, either because they are resolved informally or are filtered out as being outside the P.C.'s jurisdiction. As the limits of the P.C.'s jurisdiction are imprecise, it is possible for him to use the screening process to match complaints to the resources he has available.

If the P.C. decides to conduct an investigation, he must, under section 7(1), give the department concerned the opportunity of commenting on any allegations made. The investigation is conducted in private by a member of his staff. There are wide powers of investigation, a right to question ministers and civil servants, a right to look at all necessary documents. The right to go into the department in question and examine files is of considerable value. He is denied access only to Cabinet Papers, a restriction which the P.C. has said is no real practical hindrance. The duty to assist him overrides any obligation to maintain secrecy under the Official Secrets Acts. Under section 11, the Minister can give the P.C. notice that the publication of certain information would be prejudicial to the interests of the state. The Minister cannot, however, veto the investigation.

The case of *R. v. Parliamentary Commissioner for Administration, ex p. Dyer* (D.C., 1994) illustrates the reluctance of the courts to review the way the P.C. carries out his functions. Only in extreme cases of abuse of power might they intervene. They were, in general, unwilling to interfere with the exercise of his discretion.

The result of the investigation

The Commissioner sends a report to the M.P., the principal officer of the department investigated and any other person concerned. If indeed maladministration has been established, the report will suggest what action might be taken to remedy it. Sometimes this may be a financial payment, sometimes that a decision be reversed, sometimes an apology. (See, for example, the ex gratia payments made by the Government following the Commissioner's Report on the *Barlow Clowes* case.)

The P.C. does not have any direct sanction. He cannot enforce his recommendations. Under section 10(3) he may, however, lay a special report before Parliament. He is then dependent on the weight of opinion pressurising the department in question to comply with his recommendations.

As well as suggesting a remedy for the individual complainant, the Commissioner is equally concerned to suggest administrative changes which would prevent the occurrence of maladministration in the future.

Assessment

The Parliamentary Commissioner remains a little-known figure whose reports attract minimal publicity. Although the number of complaints has risen by about 70% over the last two years, this is from an average of around 1000, a much smaller number than anticipated and fewer per head of population than received by ombudsmen abroad. Only a small proportion of these are investigated, around 75 per cent being outside his jurisdiction or time barred. The many limitations on his jurisdiction noted above and his lack of sanction both serve to limit his effectiveness. He cannot be approached directly and he has no power to initiate investigations.

Nevertheless he has had considerable success in persuading departments to change their administrative procedures although the caution of many of his recommendations may be determined by what he knows he can achieve. A continual tension is whether he should concentrate his resources on obtaining redress in individual cases or should he devote his time to improving general standards of administration?

THE NEED FOR A BILL OF RIGHTS

Because of the extreme flexibility of our constitution, it is easy for power to shift almost imperceptibly from one body to another. It is easy for individual rights and freedoms to be eroded without the public being alerted. The traditional checks on the activities of Government appear to be singularly ineffective. The judges have, on a number of occasions, recently indicated their unwillingness to become involved in policy matters for fear of compromising their impartiality or subverting the functions of Parliament or the Executive. There have also been a number of occasions where English law has been found wanting in terms of the International Convention of Human Rights. For all these reasons there have been a number of attempts to introduce a Bill of Rights into our law—often based on the European Convention of Human Rights.

Not surprisingly none of these has received wholehearted government support as no government willingly wishes to curtail its freedom of action or limit its power. Apart from such political considerations a number of objections have been raised to the introduction of a Bill of Rights.

1.   It would alter the balance of power—from Government to the courts. If we had an entrenched Bill of Rights Parliament would no longer be supreme. The courts would have the power to interpret the Bill and to measure Parliament's subsequent actions against it. The role of the judge would be paramount. Yet to whom are our judges accountable? Any form of written constitution would inevitably increase the involvement of our judges in political controversy. Is this desirable?

2.   There would be undoubted difficulties in reaching agreement on the content of such a document. Would its content be sufficiently precise to provide any real remedy. Would there be any value in expressing the constitution in terms of broad principles?

3.   Would such a document have any value if it were not entrenched? How could it be given a higher status than other laws and protected against express and implied repeal?

Various suggestions have been made to circumvent this problem.

  (i) It has been suggested that a clause be inserted in the Bill of Rights stating that it has precedence over other Acts as occurred in Canada. (See also section 2(4) of the European Communities Act 1972.) The courts would then, it is said, interpret all laws in accordance with the Bill of Rights. But would this really lead to a different result from that in *Ellen Street Estates v. Minister of Health* (C.A., 1934) and protect against express or implied repeal?

  (ii) The Bill of Rights could be approved by referendum following the dissolution of Parliament. The new Parliament would have a moral obligation to uphold it. But this would not make successive Parliaments any less sovereign. Would the moral obligation fade?

  (iii) Professor H. W. R. Wade has argued that, as entrenchment depends entirely on the attitude of the judges, if one changes the rules by which they recognise laws as valid, one achieves effective entrenchment. If validity of legislation depends not only on its being properly passed by Parliament but also on its being in compliance with the Bill of Rights, effective entrenchment has been achieved. Wade argues that this might happen through the passage of time but that the process could be speeded up by a change in the judicial oath. Judges would swear to uphold only those laws which were properly passed and were in accordance with the Bill of Rights.

  (iv) Some writers have argued that written constitutions can prevent change by allowing minority groups to stand in the way of progress. Examples cited include the delay in giving Swiss women the vote and problems in the Republic of Ireland in relation to divorce reform, abortion law reform etc. Dicey's objection to a Bill of Rights was that a Bill of Rights could easily be suspended, that our rights arose from a variety of sources and such a network of rights was much more difficult to abolish in one stroke—the "eggs in one basket" argument.

What would be the advantages of a Bill of Rights?

  (i) It would make the law more accessible. It would publicise existing rights and increase public awareness of these rights, perhaps even stimulating a more positive interest in the content of such rights.

  (ii) Increased certainty—although a Bill of Rights would be open to interpretation.

  (iii) Would it be more difficult politically to erode rights protected in a Bill of Rights? Would the form give the rights a psychological significance? Certainly abolition of the Bill would generate publicity.

  (iv) The formulation of the Bill would provoke discussion of rights and the relationship between the various organs of Government and an examination of the effectiveness of the various safeguards.

(v) Ideally it would avoid the embarrassment of an application to an international court and hopefully provide a quicker remedy for those whose rights have been adversely affected.

---

8. SAMPLE QUESTIONS AND MODEL ANSWERS

It should be assumed that questions are answered in 45 minutes under examination conditions.

Question 1
Assess whether our present constitutional arrangements are effective in ensuring that governments act in accordance with fundamental constitutional principles. How could this effectiveness be increased?

Answer
It could be argued that amongst our most fundamental constitutional principles are:

1. Concept of legitimacy of government actions—these must be authorised by regular law, not simply by the fact that the Government is the Government.
2. The Supremacy of Parliament—Parliament is the ultimate authority.
3. The role of the judge is to interpret the law, not to create it.
4. The protection of individual rights.

Our present constitutional arrangements may be lacking in ensuring governments act in accordance with these.

1. Lack of a written, entrenched constitution
(i) Our unwritten, flexible constitution does not delimit the power of the Government. This area of law is largely regulated by convention. Conventions evolve. The Government in power has opportunity to shape conventions to their advantage.
(ii) The inherent flexibility allows changes to be made without alerting the public. No normal steps need be taken. It has been argued, for example, that rights of peaceful process were weakened by recent legislation without prior public debate.
(iii) The judiciary do not have a framework within which to operate in attempting to control abuse of power.

2. In theory Parliament is supreme

In practice this means the Government. Our first past the post electoral system means that governments may not have a majority of votes cast in an election. Nevertheless once elected it could act contrary to the rule of law with no legal checks.

(i)   We have a Constitutional Monarchy.
(ii) The power of the House of Lords is limited by the Parliament Acts 1911–49, its lack of credibility arising from its composition, and its fear of abolition.
(iii) The courts (except in the context of the E.U.) have been unwilling to challenge the validity of an Act of Parliament (reference *Pickin*'s case.)
(iv) The Government can largely control the Commons—through its majority, the Whip System, Patronage, Control of the timetable.

Suggestions for increasing effectiveness have included:

(i)   A written constitution and a bill of rights.
(ii) Electoral reform.
(iii) Stronger checks and balances within the system, *e.g.* wider distribution of power through the federal system.

These should be briefly assessed.

Question 2

Geoff, an M.P., receives a letter from a constituent alleging that Marty Muddle, the Chief Executive of a Government Agency has been receiving bribes. Geoff writes to the appropriate minister raising the issue and sending a copy of his letter to Marty for his comments.

In a speech to his constituency association, Geoff refers to the allegations that have been made, indicating that he intends to promote legislation in the current parliamentary session to make such executives more accountable. As a result of the publicity, questions are asked in the House during which further allegations are made against Marty by Geoff.

The Daily Scandal reports the matter, both in its Parliamentary Report and also, briefly, in a "parliamentary sketch."

Advise Marty.

Answer

Marty may wish to bring an action of defamation against Geoff and against the Daily Scandal. The question is whether and to what extent they are protected by parliamentary privilege.

The action against Geoff

M.P.'s have absolute privilege in regard to words spoken in the course of Parliamentary proceedings and qualified privilege in relation to words spoken in the course of their duties. The nature of absolute and qualified privilege should be explained indicating the extent of the protection given by each.

The letter to the Minister

Whether this is covered by absolute privilege depends on its being considered "a proceeding before Parliament." (Article 9 of the Bill of Rights.) A parallel should be drawn with the *Strauss* Case (1958) where the House of Commons rejected the view of the Committee on Privileges that correspondence between an M.P. and a Minister on a matter of public concern attracted absolute privilege and resolved that the M.P. was protected only in so far as he had acted in good faith and without malice.

Parliament is not however bound by such resolutions and it should be noted that the Committee on Privileges has recommended on several occasions since then that such communications be accorded absolute privilege, particularly if the matter will come before the House in the current session. It appears that the matter has been raised before the House during question time.

Thus if it is a proceeding before Parliament, no action can be brought (*Church of Scientology of California v. Johnson-Smith* (1972)). If it is found not to be a proceeding before Parliament, G can be sued although he may have a defence of qualified privilege as the minister has an interest in this matter as being of public concern (*Beach v. Freesom* (1972)). It should, however, be considered whether publishing the allegation without first checking the facts constitutes malice.

The speech to the constituency association

Following *R. v. Creevey* (1813), if allegations covered by absolute privilege are repeated outside Parliament, an action of defamation can lie. *Davison v. Duncan* (1857) suggests that it is doubtful if qualified privilege would be granted to G if he repeats the allegations simply for the information of his constituents.

The questions in the House

These would appear to be "proceedings before Parliament" (Erskine May and the Select Committee on Privileges 1938) and as such they attract absolute privilege and no action can lie.

The Daily Scandal

Newspapers reporting Parliamentary Affairs may be protected against actions of defamation:

(a) Under the Parliamentary Papers Act 1840 which gives absolute protection to all papers published by order of Parliament and copies of such papers (ss.1 and 2) and qualified privilege to extracts from such papers published in good faith and without malice (s.3).

(b) Reports of public meetings, including meetings of Parliament, attract qualified privilege providing the report is fair and accurate, in good faith and without malice and publication is deemed to be for the benefit of the public.

The source of the Daily Scandal report is unclear. It is unlikely to take the form of an extract from Hansard and so section 3 of the 1840 Act will give no protection. If based on a report of a public meeting it may attract qualified privilege if fair and accurate unless Marty can prove malice.

The fairness of the report does not depend on its completeness. Even a selective report, providing it is balanced, may be deemed to be fair. (*Cook v. Alexander* 1973). Thus even the parliamentary sketch may attract qualified privilege as in *Cook*'s case.

Parliamentary remedies

It could be noted briefly that although no remedy is obtained against either party in court, Marty may have the satisfaction of seeing action being taken against Geoff for contempt of Parliament if it is felt that he has abused his privilege of free speech. This is unlikely in view of Parliament's lack of response in situations such as the naming of Colonel B contrary to the wishes of the court. A newspaper may also be in contempt of Parliament if it prints anything which brings the House into disrepute.

Question 3

One evening the police receive reports that two youths have stolen cigarettes and some money from an old age pensioner who had just bought them at a local corner shop. He described them as quite small, wearing dark shell suits and one had a red baseball cap. Half an hour later PC Smith sees three boys smoking outside the shop. They are known to him as "troublemakers". They are all wearing shell suits but none are wearing caps.

He orders them to turn out their pockets which they grudgingly do. Nothing untoward is found. While the search is taking place, one of the youths ostentatiously drops a crisp packet on the ground at the officer's feet. He refuses to pick it up and tells the officer what to do with the crisp packet!

At this point the officer bundles the youth into a police car and tells him he is under arrest. Consider the legality of the police conduct.

Answer

1. Consider whether PC Smith has the power to order the youths to turn out their pockets?

   (i)   There may be a power to stop and search for stolen goods under s.1 (2) (a) of PACE 1984.

  (ii)   The officer must have reasonable grounds for suspecting that he will find stolen goods (s.1 (3)).

 (iii)   Para.1 of the Code of Practice on Stop and Search emphasises that whether the police have reasonable grounds for the stop and search depends on the circumstances of the case but they must have an objective basis, *i.e.* one which would appear justifiable and reasonable to a third party. Thus PC Smith can rely on the description of the alleged offenders, their presence in the vicinity, their demeanour. He can take into account his knowledge of them in conjunction with the other information noted above. He cannot rely on personal factors alone (Code para. 1.7), *e.g.* their bad reputation plus appearing a stereotyped offender.

 (iv)   Juveniles should not be subject to a voluntary search (Code Note 1G).

You should reach a conclusion on this noting that the fact nothing was found is irrelevant. It was whether the officer had reasonable grounds at the time he embarked on the search.

2. Assuming there was a power to stop and search has the search been carried out properly in terms of the Act?

   (i)   The search should be carried out courteously (Code Note 1(a)).

  (ii)   If PC Smith is not in uniform, he must supply documentary evidence, s.2 (2) (b).

 (iii)   He should have provided the information required in s.2 (3).

 (iv)   Having carried out the search, PC Smith should have completed a record of the search in accordance with s.3 and recorded the information required in s.3 (6). There appears to be no reason to exclude this requirement under s.3 (1) or to delay making it under s.3 (2).

  (v)   The power would entitle the police officer to ask the boys to turn out their pockets. He has not infringed s.2 (9) (a).

It appears that while the extent of the search was lawful, the formalities which are designed to protect suspects have not been complied with.

3. The validity of the "arrest"—the grounds?

   (i)   Note that the police have a summary power of arrest under ss. 24 and 25 of PACE and at common law to prevent the continuance of a breach of the peace. No arrestable offence appears to have been committed. (You may choose to define this.) Most likely power under s.25.

(ii) Examine the s.25 power noting that the constable must suspect that an offence must have been committed etc., and that service of a summons would be impracticable or inappropriate because one of the general arrest conditions applies. Examine the general arrest conditions in s.25 (3) and consider whether any of these apply to this situation and conclude whether there are legal grounds for the arrest.

4. Have the formalities been complied with for a valid arrest?

(i) The youth has been informed that he is under arrest—s.28 (1).

(ii) He has not been informed of the grounds of the arrest s.28 (3). This is required even if the facts are obvious—s.28 (4). There appears to be no justification for delaying the giving of this information in accordance with s.28 (5).

(iii) Consider whether the officer has used unjustifiable force.

Conclusion

Question 4

Sam earns a living by selling ice-cream from a van in the city of Oldtown. In May 1980 Oldtown City Council opened a Leisure Centre which, among other things, sells ice-cream and soft drinks. Sam sells ice-cream from his van outside the Leisure Centre every Saturday and Sunday afternoon. On Saturday August 9, Sam is told to move his ice-cream van away by an official of the Leisure Centre. He refuses in no uncertain language and the following day sells ice-cream there as usual. On Tuesday August 12 he receives a letter from Oldtown City Council telling Sam that his licence to sell ice-cream is revoked as from Friday August 15.

Sam appeals against this decision. No reasons are given for removing his licence, but Sam is told he can appear in person before a special meeting of the Licence Appeals Committee on Monday August 18. He is refused legal representation at the hearing and is prevented by the chairman from cross-examining witnesses. The decision to remove Sam's licence is confirmed by the Appeals Committee whose Chairman is manager of the Oldtown Leisure Centre.

Advise Sam.

Answer

Consider the possibility of applying for judicial review of the decision to remove Sam's licence on ground of procedural impropriety.

1. Is there an implied requirement that the decision is taken fairly in accordance with the rules of natural justice?

(a) Note that this is a licensing decision which has been analysed as relating to a privilege and that traditionally natural justice applied to decisions affecting legal rights—*R. v. Electricity Commissioners, ex p. London Electricity Joint Committee.*

(b) Consideration of how natural justice was applied in a wider range of circumstances—the development of *Ridge v. Baldwin*—a right, interest or legitimate expectation of a hearing.

(c) The application of natural justice to licensing cases—*McInnes v. Onslow Fane and ex p. Hook*—revocation of existing licences. Note that the legitimate expectation of being given a fair hearing may arise from:

being deprived of an existing licence
the right to answer allegations
the seriousness of the consequences.

2. Has there been a breach of the nemo judex rule?

(a) Although the connection appears too remote to amount to a direct pecuniary interest, the Chairman may have a non-pecuniary interest through his business connection with the Leisure Centre and possibly through acting as complainant and judge.

(b) Consider and apply the appropriate test of bias.

3. Consider whether S has been given a fair hearing

(a) Has he been adequately informed of the complaint against him?

(b) Does fairness demand legal representation in the circumstances and a right to cross-examine witnesses? (Note the requirement of equality of treatment between the parties.)

Question 5

The office of Parliamentary Commissioner for Administration was established to provide a remedy for the citizen who has suffered as a result of maladministration by central government. What advantages does this have over pre-existing judicial and parliamentary remedies? In what ways could the Parliamentary Commissioner's effectiveness be increased?

Answer

Prior to the establishment of the office of Parliamentary Commissioner in 1967, the citizen complaining of maladministration could either:

(a) complain to an M.P.;

(b) pursue a legal remedy in the courts.

The Critchel Down Affair illustrated the limitations of these methods. The P.C. appears to have certain advantages.

Advantage over M.P.'s action

1. The P.C. is not hampered by any political allegiance but is independent.

2. The P.C. has greater ability to determine how the decision was reached.

Note. His powers of investigation (s.7). M.P.s may question ministers but have limited power and opportunity to force the minister to disclose more than he wishes. The *Sachsenhausen Concentration Camp* case illustrates the way in which the P.C.'s wider powers of investigation prove more effective, in particular his right of access to departmental files and the fact that he is not restricted by the Official Secrets Acts.

Advantage over judicial remedies

1. The P.C. investigates complaints of maladministration. The meaning of this term should be discussed and it should be noted that it is wider than the range of administrative defects open to investigation by the courts who can intervene only:

(a) where there is a breach of the rules of natural justice;
(b) where the decision is *ultra vires*;
(c) where there is an error of law on the face of the record;
(d) where there is a statutory right of appeal.

Although the involvement of the courts in administrative decision making has increased in recent years as a result of:

(a) the extension of the application of the rules of natural justice to a wider range of situations;
(b) the development of the concept of abuse of power and the increased control of the courts over discretionary decision making; the courts cannot be said to provide a comprehensive review of the activities of the administration.

2. The court is concerned with giving a remedy to the individual applicant. The Parliamentary Commissioner is also concerned with improving the general standard of administration in the department in question.

3. The court will reach its decision on the basis of the evidence presented to it by the parties. The Crown may even attempt to rely on public interest immunity to prevent information being made available. Contrast this with the wide investigative powers of the P.C.

It should, of course, be noted that where there is a legal remedy the P.C. will not normally investigate.

The P.C.'s effectiveness could be increased in the following ways:

1. By increasing his jurisdiction:

(a) By expanding the definition of "maladministration" to enable him to investigate "any unreasonable, unjust or oppressive action. "

(b) By removing the restrictions in Schedule 3, *e.g.* by allowing the P.C. to investigate contractual and commercial matters involving government departments.

(c) By allowing the P.C. to investigate more freely disputes where there might also be a legal remedy.

2. By making him more accessible:

(a) Discuss the possibility of removing the M.P. filter.

(b) Consider how public awareness of his role might be increased, noting the low level of complaints presently investigated.

3. By giving the P.C. an effective sanction. Describe his present powers to ensure his recommendations are implemented. These could be contrasted with those of the Northern Ireland Commissioner.

4. By allowing him to initiate investigations.

INDEX